McGraw-Hill's

CAREERS FOR

SCHOLARS

& Other Deep Thinkers

D0976566

Careers for You Series

McGraw-Hill's

CAREERS FOR

SCHOLARS

& Other Deep Thinkers

BLYTHE CAMENSON

SECOND EDITION

New York Chicago San Francisco Lisbon London Madrid Mexico City
Milan New Delhi San Juan Seoul Singapore Sydney Toronto

The *McGraw·Hill* Companies

Library of Congress Cataloging-in-Publication Data

Camenson, Blythe.
  Careers for scholars and other deep thinkers / by Blythe Camenson — 2nd ed.
    p.   cm. — (McGraw-Hill careers for you series)
  Includes bibliographical references.
  ISBN 0-07-149316-6 (alk. paper)
    1. Vocational guidance—United States. 2. Learning and scholarship.
  I. Title.

  HF5382.5.U5C25193 2008
  331.702'35—dc22   2008005199

1 2 3 4 5 6 7 8 9 10 11 12 13 14 15 16 17 18 19   DOC/DOC   0 9 8

ISBN 978-0-07-149316-1
MHID   0-07-149316-6

McGraw-Hill books are available at special quantity discounts to use as premiums and sales promotions or for use in corporate training programs. To contact a representative, please visit the Contact Us pages at www.mhprofessional.com.

This book is printed on acid-free paper.

To all my university professors,
who guided me and
satisfied my curiosity

Contents

	Acknowledgments	ix
CHAPTER ONE	**Studying the Options**	1
CHAPTER TWO	**College and University Professors**	7
CHAPTER THREE	**Librarians and Archivists**	21
CHAPTER FOUR	**Social Scientists**	41
CHAPTER FIVE	**Archaeologists**	55
CHAPTER SIX	**Psychologists**	67
CHAPTER SEVEN	**Museum Curators**	87
CHAPTER EIGHT	**Botanical Specialists**	105
CHAPTER NINE	**Animal Behaviorists**	119
CHAPTER TEN	**Researchers, Writers, and Genealogists**	129
APPENDIX	**Professional Associations**	143

Acknowledgments

The author would like to thank the following scholars and other deep thinkers for providing information about their careers.

Anne Brennan	Student Intern
Susan Broadwater-Chen	Information Specialist and Freelance Writer
Judy Burns	Adjunct Lecturer
Marshall J. Cook	Professor
Rick Darke	Curator of Plants
John Fleckner	Chief Archivist
Ann Gardner	Social Anthropologist
Erica Hirshler	Curator of Paintings
Carol Jones	Technical Services Librarian
Susan Kelley	Curatorial Associate
Kristin Kuckelman	Senior Archaeologist
Charles McGovern	Curator
Valarie Neiman	Academic Researcher
Mary Lee Nitschke	Animal Behaviorist
Steve Oserman	Reference Librarian
Gerald D. Oster	Clinical Psychologist
Clay Reynolds	Novelist
Chris Strand	Outreach Horticulturist
Denise Stybr	School Psychologist
Carolyn Travers	Director of Research
Jill Winland-Brown	Professor of Nursing

The author also wishes to thank Josephine Scanlon for her assistance in preparing this revision.

McGraw-Hill's

CAREERS FOR

SCHOLARS

& Other Deep Thinkers

CHAPTER ONE

Studying the Options

Many students wait impatiently for their final year of school. For them, graduation marks not only the beginning of an exciting new time of life, but perhaps more importantly, the end of school, studying, and research.

Then there are those like you, who truly delight in the scholastic life. You feel comfortable in a classroom, enjoying a lecture or the give and take of a spirited discussion. You gain satisfaction from research, poring through old volumes in the library stacks, searching the Internet for just the right materials, and assembling a well-written paper.

The years that you have spent working on your undergraduate degree have been devoted to preparing yourself not for a jump into the real world but for another round of educational pursuit. The world of academia is your calling, and, whether your goal is to stay within those hallowed halls or move into a comparable setting, *Careers for Scholars* will introduce you to a variety of choices to suit your degree and interests.

Do You Have What It Takes?

What is a scholar? The dictionary defines it as a learned or erudite person, an individual who is educated and well-read, an intellectual and a thinker. A scholar is also a student, pursuing knowledge for its own sake and to pass it on to others.

Scholars are often experts in a particular body of knowledge—the contemporary American novel, for example, or the culture of the Kalahari Bushmen in the deserts of Africa. They can be sociologists, historians, anthropologists, archaeologists, psychologists, animal behaviorists, botanists, horticulturists, museum curators, librarians, archivists, or teachers—or they can work in a score of other academic and professional pursuits.

Although their academic training may vary, they share many of the same skills and interests. Scholars are excellent researchers, spending a great deal of time perusing reference books, periodicals, abstracts, and the Internet to solve their latest research puzzles.

Many scholars are also excellent teachers. Through their research and academic studies, they have become immersed in particular disciplines and are able to pass on their knowledge to others, whether through classroom interaction, talks and presentations, the written word, or any combination thereof. But teaching, research, and writing are not the only ways in which scholars use their skills and talents to earn a living. Though most are thrilled by the discoveries of research, others are collectors or catalogers by nature. Whatever your particular scholarly interest, you will find almost as many settings in which to work as areas of study to pursue.

Settings for Scholars

Universities and colleges are the most obvious settings, and it is true that a wide range of research and teaching does go on within those ivy-covered walls. However, scholars also find employment in the following settings:

- archives
- libraries
- museums

- botanical gardens
- zoos
- laboratories
- hospitals
- archaeological sites

In addition, certain scholars, such as anthropologists, sociologists, or archaeologists, conduct research in the field, in Africa, for example, or in Samoa, Papua New Guinea, and even within the shores of North America.

Throughout this book, we explore a variety of settings where you, as a job-hunting scholar, might find your niche.

Job Titles for Scholars

Many job titles are common to each particular setting, but the job description varies depending on the institution. Curators, for example, are found in virtually every kind of museum, from art and science to history museums, as well as in botanical gardens and even corporations, even though the collections they deal with and their specific duties are very different. In *Careers for Scholars*, we examine the following career designations:

- university professor
- genealogist
- museum curator
- botanical garden curator
- archaeologist
- anthropologist
- archivist
- librarian
- researcher
- psychologist
- animal behaviorist

This list is far from comprehensive—the settings and job titles for scholars can stretch to include all the different "ologies." As you set out on your job search in your own specialized area of study, you will be able to add to the suggestions here and create your own tailor-made inventory.

Heaven-Sent Jobs for Scholars

Job-hunting scholars dream of finding positions that will allow them to combine their skills and interests. Would any of these help-wanted listings have you making sure that your resume is up-to-date?

- **Researcher.** University department seeks experienced researcher for project assisting dissertation students.
- **Dig Site Assistant.** Position open for energetic student or recent graduate at major archaeological dig site in New Mexico. Duties include cleaning and recording discovered artifacts.
- **Information Officer.** Historic site preservation board has opening for officer to disseminate information to the public. Good writing skills necessary. Bilingual, Spanish/English, a plus.
- **University Instructor.** Four-year liberal arts college seeks to fill a tenure-track position in the anthropology department. Duties include classroom teaching and student advising. Research budget available.
- **Assistant Collections Manager.** Prestigious New York museum seeks master's level or above historian to work in the collection department. Knowledge of eighteenth-century European art a plus.

Do You Have the Necessary Qualifications?

The qualifications you'll need vary depending on the job. Although many employers prefer their applicants to have master's degrees or even doctorates, others are satisfied with bachelor's degrees. In some situations, the following qualifications are equally important: experience, extensive knowledge of a particular time period or region, the ability to communicate with diverse groups of people, good writing skills, and research skills.

Salaries

Salaries vary widely from position to position but are generally low, as are most pay scales for education-related fields. Factors such as the source of funding or the geographic region have more impact on salary levels than the complexity of the job or the level of the candidates' education and experience.

Some jobs pay only hourly wages; others follow the federal government's General Schedule (GS) pay scale. Most jobs provide benefits such as health insurance. But all the professional scholars showcased in the pages to come stress that financial rewards were not the main reason, or even a consideration, in pursuing their chosen professions. The low pay is far outweighed by the satisfaction of doing work they love.

The Job Hunt

Although many scholars can find employment in their own hometowns—in a local university or historic house museum, for example—you may have to relocate in order to broaden your opportunities. If you have a spot in mind where you'd like to work, a phone call or an introductory letter sent with your resume is a good way to start. If you would like some more ideas on possible locations, there are several directories listed at the end of various chapters that can lead you to interesting destinations.

Many professional associations produce monthly or quarterly newsletters with job listings and upcoming internships and fellowships. Some key addresses have also been provided for you in the Appendix.

CHAPTER TWO

College and University Professors

Perhaps no career seems quite as scholarly as teaching in a college or university. These scholars teach and advise more than sixteen million full-time and part-time college students and perform a significant part of the nation's research. They also study and meet with colleagues to keep up with developments in their fields and consult with government, business, nonprofit, and community organizations.

Faculty members generally are organized into departments or divisions, based on their subject or field. They usually teach several different courses within their departments. For example, a professor in the political science department might teach classes in American politics, political theory, and political economics. Professors may instruct undergraduate or graduate students, or both.

College and university faculty may teach classes of twenty or so students, give lectures to several hundred students in large halls, lead small seminars, and supervise students in laboratories. They also prepare lectures, exercises, and laboratory experiments; grade exams and papers; and work with students individually. Many teach and supervise graduate student research.

These scholars keep abreast of developments in their fields by reading current literature, meeting with colleagues, and participating in professional conferences. Many conduct their own research, which may include running experiments, collecting and analyzing data, or examining original documents, literature, and other source material. Based on their results, they develop hypotheses, arrive at conclusions, and write about their findings in scholarly journals and books.

Most faculty members serve on academic or administrative committees that deal with the policies of their institutions, departmental matters, academic issues, curricula, budgets, equipment purchases, and hiring. Some work with student organizations. The greatest administrative responsibilities generally fall to department heads.

Individual circumstances and the type of institution determine the amount of time faculty members spend on each of these activities. For example, those working at universities generally spend a significant part of their time doing research; those in four-year colleges, somewhat less; and those in two-year colleges, relatively little because the teaching load usually is heavier.

Most college faculty members have flexible schedules. They usually teach for twelve to sixteen hours a week, attend faculty and committee meetings, and establish regular office hours for student consultations, usually three to six hours per week. Otherwise, they are relatively free to decide when and where they work and how much time to devote to course preparation, grading papers and exams, study, research, and other activities. They may work staggered hours and teach classes at night and on weekends, particularly if they teach older students who may have full-time jobs or family responsibilities on weekdays. They have even greater flexibility during the summer and school holidays, when they may teach, do research, travel, or pursue nonacademic interests. Part-time faculty generally spend little time on campus, since most don't have an office, and some teach at more than one college.

Most colleges and universities have funds to support faculty research or other professional development needs, including travel to conferences and research sites.

Some faculty members experience a conflict between their responsibilities to teach students and the pressure to do research. This may be a particular problem for young faculty seeking advancement, who need to publish their work in order to advance their reputations. However, some of this pressure is alleviated by an increasing emphasis on undergraduate teaching performance, particularly at small liberal arts colleges.

Training

Most college and university faculty are in four academic ranks: professor, associate professor, assistant professor, and instructor. A small number are lecturers.

So, how can you achieve the scholarly position of college teacher? In general, newly hired faculty members begin as instructors or assistant professors. To work in a four-year college or university, you would generally need a doctorate for a full-time, tenure-track position. Some schools hire applicants who hold a master's degree or who are doctoral candidates for certain disciplines, such as the arts, or for part-time and temporary jobs.

You may be qualified to teach in a two-year college with a master's degree; however, competition for jobs can lead to schools being more selective, and master's degree holders may be passed over in favor of candidates with doctorates. Many two-year institutions increasingly prefer job applicants to have some teaching experience or experience with distance learning. Preference also may be given to those holding dual master's degrees, especially at smaller institutions, because they can teach more subjects.

A doctoral program takes an average of six years of full-time study beyond your bachelor's degree, including time spent completing a master's degree and a dissertation. Some programs, such as those in the humanities, may take longer to complete; others, such as those in engineering, usually are shorter. As a doctoral candidate, you will specialize in a subfield of a discipline, such as organic chemistry, counseling psychology, or European history, but will also take courses covering the entire discipline.

A typical program includes twenty or more increasingly specialized courses and seminars plus comprehensive examinations on all major areas of the field. You will be required to complete a dissertation, which is a written report based on original research in your major field of study. The dissertation sets forth an original hypothesis or proposes a model and tests it. Students in the natural sciences and engineering usually do laboratory work; in the humanities, they study original documents and other published material. Your dissertation will be done under the guidance of one or more faculty advisors and may take one or two years of full-time work.

After earning their degrees, some students, particularly those in the natural sciences, spend additional years on postdoctoral research and study before taking a faculty position. Some Ph.D.s are able to extend postdoctoral appointments or take new ones, if they are unable to find a faculty job. Most postdoctoral appointments offer a nominal salary.

Obtaining a position as a graduate teaching assistant is an excellent way to gain college teaching experience. To qualify, you must be enrolled in a graduate school program, and some colleges and universities require you to attend classes or take some training prior to being given responsibility for a course.

Graduate teaching assistants usually work at the institution and in the department where they are earning their degrees. However, teaching or internship positions for graduate students at institutions that do not grant a graduate degree have become more common in recent years. For example, a program called Preparing Future Faculty, administered by the Association of American Colleges and Universities and the Council of Graduate Schools, has led to the creation of many now-independent programs that offer graduate students at research universities the opportunity to work as teaching assistants at other types of institutions, such as liberal arts or community colleges. In this situation, you would work with a mentor while teaching classes and learning how to improve your teaching techniques. You may also be expected to attend faculty and committee meetings, develop a curriculum, and learn how to balance the teaching, research, and administrative roles that faculty play. You can gain valuable experience in teaching at the postsecondary level and also explore the differences among the various types of institutions at which you may someday work.

Attaining tenure is a major step in the traditional academic career. Newly hired faculty serve a certain period (usually seven years) under term contracts. Then, their records of teaching, research, and overall contributions to the institution and the field are reviewed; tenure is granted if the review is favorable and positions are available. A tenured professor cannot be fired without just cause and due process. Those denied tenure usually must leave the institution.

Tenure protects the faculty's academic freedom, the ability to teach and conduct research without fear of being fired for advocating unpopular ideas. It also gives both faculty and institutions the stability needed for effective research and teaching and provides financial stability for faculty members. About 60 percent of full-time faculty are tenured, and many others are in the probationary period.

Some faculty advance into administrative and managerial positions, such as departmental chairperson, dean, and president. Such a promotion is based on teaching experience, research, publication, and service on campus committees and task forces. At four-year institutions, this advancement requires a doctoral degree.

Job Outlook

Job prospects for college and university teachers are good. Overall, employment in this area is expected to increase 27 percent or more through 2014. A significant proportion of these new jobs will be part-time positions, and opportunities will vary somewhat from field to field, as numerous openings for all types of post-secondary teachers result from retirements of current teachers and continued increases in student enrollments.

The projected growth in college and university enrollment over the next decade stems mainly from an increase in the population of eighteen- to twenty-four-year-olds and from the increasing number of high school graduates who choose to attend these institutions. Adults returning to college to enhance their career prospects or to update their skills also will continue to create new opportunities for teachers, particularly at community colleges and for-profit institutions that cater to working adults.

However, many postsecondary educational institutions receive a significant portion of their funding from state and local governments, so expansion of public higher education will be limited by budgetary restrictions. Nevertheless, in addition to growth in enrollments, the need to replace the large numbers of teachers who are likely to retire over the next decade will also create a significant number of openings. Many of the postsecondary teachers hired in the late 1960s and the 1970s to teach baby boomers are expected to retire in growing numbers in the years ahead.

The outlook is favorable for Ph.D. recipients seeking jobs over the next decade. Although competition will remain tight for tenure-track positions at four-year colleges and universities, a considerable number of part-time or renewable term appointments at these institutions and positions at community colleges should be available. Opportunities for master's degree holders are also expected to be favorable, as community colleges and other institutions, such as professional career education programs, are expected to experience considerable growth.

Opportunities for graduate teaching assistants are expected to be very good due to prospects for much higher undergraduate enrollments coupled with more modest graduate enrollment increases. Constituting almost 9 percent of all postsecondary teachers, graduate teaching assistants play an integral role in the postsecondary education system, and they are expected to continue to do so in the future.

Since one of the main reasons why students attend postsecondary institutions is to prepare themselves for careers, the best job prospects for postsecondary teachers are likely to be in fields where job growth is expected to be strong over the next decade. These include fields such as business, health specialties, nursing, and biological sciences. Community colleges and other institutions offering career and technical education have been among the most rapidly growing, and these institutions are expected to offer some of the best opportunities for postsecondary teachers.

Salaries

Earnings for college faculty vary according to rank and type of institution, geographic area, and field. According to a 2004–2005 survey by the American Association of University Professors, salaries for full-time faculty averaged $68,505. By rank, the average was $91,548 for professors, $65,113 for associate professors, $54,571 for assistant professors, $39,899 for instructors, and $45,647 for lecturers. Faculty in four-year institutions earn higher salaries, on average, than do those in two-year schools.

In 2004–2005, faculty salaries averaged $79,342 in private independent institutions, $66,851 in public institutions, and $61,103 in religiously affiliated private colleges and universities. In fields with high-paying nonacademic alternatives, such as medicine, law, engineering, and business, among others, earnings exceed these averages. In others fields, such as the humanities and education, they are lower.

Many faculty members have significant earnings in addition to the base salary, whether from consulting, teaching additional courses, working on research projects, writing for publication, or taking other employment. In addition, many enjoy some unique benefits, including access to campus facilities, tuition waivers for dependents, housing and travel allowances, and paid sabbatical leaves. Part-time faculty usually have fewer benefits than full-time faculty.

Profiles

What better way to get a feel for a particular career path or job setting than to hear from a professional actively working in the field. The following three university teachers provide an inside view of academia.

Jill Winland-Brown—Professor of Nursing

Jill Winland-Brown is a nurse and a doctor—a doctor of education—who teaches future nurses at Florida Atlantic University in Boca Raton, Florida. She has been a registered nurse (R.N.) for more than thirty years and a university professor for twenty. She earned her R.N. in a three-year diploma program. After working for seven years, she returned to school to earn her bachelor's, then her master's, and, finally, her doctorate. She worked as a nurse throughout her studies.

The Work. Jill describes her work as having three components: teaching, service, and research. She teaches clinical and theory courses such as nursing ethics, leadership management, and technological skills (giving medications, starting IVs, and so forth) twelve hours a week. In addition, she prepares lessons and grades assignments.

The service portion of her job involves giving something back to the community and to the university. In this capacity, she serves on a number of boards and committees and advises both undergraduate and graduate students and helps them with independent studies or with their theses or dissertations.

The third component, research, is expected of a professor to further her own knowledge and that of others in important areas. Some of her research topics have involved problems for disabled nurses and summer camp nursing. She writes papers that report her findings and submits them to professional journals for publication.

She feels that she does a little of each—teaching, service, and research—every day. What Jill loves most about her work is watching her students learn and mature and then go on to find rewarding careers. She enjoys working with a wide range of students, whether they're freshmen, seniors, master's students, or R.N.s coming back to earn their bachelor's degrees.

As an advisor, she works with students who are assigned to her when they begin their studies and stay with her throughout their programs. She likes being able to follow them through their educations and to get to know them well.

In addition, Jill enjoys being near people who are working in a variety of disciplines. Most hospital nurses work only with other health care professionals, but in a university setting, she comes in contact with people involved in many kinds of work.

Although she believes strongly in giving back to the university, the committee work takes a lot of time. And as a university professor, she also faces the pressure of "publish or perish." Professors are expected to write articles and have them published in professional journals—in many cases, a teacher's continued research funding depends on these publications. "You might spend a lot of time on two different papers," Jill says. "One gets published right away, and the other you might have to submit several times, but they're both of equal value. It takes a lot of time."

Judy Burns—Adjunct Lecturer

Judy Burns teaches screenwriting classes at UCLA Extension and in UCLA's master of fine arts program. She has had an extensive career in television, including writing for shows such as "Star Trek," "Mission Impossible," "The Fugitive," "Magnum, P.I.,"

"Vegas," "T.J. Hooker," "Marcus Welby, M.D.," "Lucas Tanner," and "MacGyver." She also teaches screenwriting classes on America Online.

Judy spends six hours in the classroom each week, teaching two classes. She also keeps office hours and usually spends a few hours a week meeting with students. Preparation and grading also add to her schedule; for a three-hour class, she puts in an additional six hours.

She teaches a graduate course called Polishing Your Script in UCLA's School of Theater, Film, and Television. It's the first time the program has offered a class in rewriting, and Judy was asked to teach it because of her work in the Extension program.

She enjoys the constant contact with the students, saying, "I find that writers who work in a little room sometimes become too introspective and don't maintain contact with humanity—which is what they need to write and talk about. The constant influx of new ideas is great—you absorb all of that."

The only downside is that teaching takes time away from her own writing and forces her to set aside specific time to do her own work. But other than that, she's very happy with her teaching job.

Getting Started. Judy has a bachelor of arts degree in anthropology from the University of California, Irvine, and a master's with an interdisciplinary major in theater, English, and history from Cal State in San Bernardino. She also earned a doctorate in critical studies in theater at UCLA.

She worked her way up through Hollywood as a story editor and producer, so she learned these skills from some talented people. In that position, she was on the other side of the desk every day listening to writers who came to sell her their stories. After a while, she decided that it was time to pass on all of the information she had accumulated. However, she realized that in order to pass it on properly, she needed to understand the roots of screenwriting. Judy says that she became a screenwriter basically to earn money. She was an anthropology student at the time, saving for a ticket to Africa to work on an anthropological dig.

"And here I was suddenly selling, then on staff," she says. "I was a writer, but I'd never had any academic training for it. I was a transplanted anthropologist. It's not a bad background, that and psychology, but I'd never had Shakespeare courses or drama or read a Tennessee Williams play. But I had a knack for writing, and I had read all my life."

All of Judy's screenwriting credits are in television. Her break came with "Star Trek," and the episode she wrote, called "The Tholian Web," won an Emmy for special effects.

"I don't want to disillusion young people, but I had managed to work consistently for twenty years and then decided to go back to school and teach what I know. I'd rather be poor and refreshed, constantly in contact with students. There comes a time when you have to give it back and fill up your own container. After twenty years, I felt depleted. By going back to school, I had the time to read and then took teaching assistant positions and was suddenly in contact with young people, and my universe expanded beyond just television. What I found was that the more I read, the more I absorbed, and I then almost immediately began to teach these things. I learned to appreciate teaching as an art form."

Advice from a Professional. Judy says that in order to become an instructor, you need a solid history of working in a particular profession, or you need to get at least a master's degree, if not a doctorate. You must be willing to invest the time to accomplish this, because a bachelor's degree won't get you very far.

Marshall J. Cook—Professor

Marshall J. Cook is a full professor in the department of communication programs, part of the division of continuing studies at the University of Wisconsin, Madison. He is also a writer with hundreds of articles to his credit, a couple of dozen short stories, and numerous books, including *Writing for the Joy of It, Freeing Your Creativity: A Writer's Guide, How to Write with the Skill of a Master and the Genius of a Child, Slow Down and Get More Done, Leads & Conclusions*, and *Hometown Wisconsin*.

Before coming to Wisconsin, he worked for eight years as an instructor at Solano Community College in Suisun City, California. Marshall describes his current position as different from that of the traditional campus teacher. The Division of Continuing Studies is a separate unit within the university with the primary mission of adult education. He conducts workshops and does some consulting and on-site training of newspaper people and corporate communicators. For example, he runs a media workshop for police officers called Preparing to Be Interviewed by the Press, one on newsletter preparation, and another on stress management that follows his book, *Slow Down and Get More Done*.

Marshall says, "Basically, I offer anything we can sell to the public. We're an income-generating unit, unlike campus teaching, and we're responsible for paying our own way."

In this capacity, he develops the workshops and also helps to publicize them in addition to his teaching duties. Each year he teaches between sixty and seventy workshops and also does guest speaking engagements and helps out at other conferences. While this might sound like quite a heavy workload, Marshall points out that there is no research component to his job. His research is all practical, and his publications are all mass media because that's what he teaches.

The work is diverse and offers a rare opportunity to combine writing with another career that complements it. As he says, "The writing helps me teach, and the teaching helps me write."

Although the work is stimulating, he admits that it can be very tiring. Marshall does a lot of traveling to conduct workshops, and sometimes he does as many as three in a week.

Getting Started. Marshall has a B.A. in creative writing and an M.A. in communications and print journalism from Stanford

University. He attended law school for about four months but realized that although he enjoyed studying the law, he wasn't interested in the actual day-to-day work of practice. He taught one English class at the University of Santa Clara in California and was hired full-time when a position became available. Marshall worked in the English department for four years and found himself thoroughly enjoying his job, remembering that his dream had always been to be a teacher and writer.

He began working as a member of the academic staff at the University of Wisconsin in 1979 as a program coordinator. Marshall acknowledges that he's among the last people who entered the system in this way, moving from the academic staff track to a tenure-track position. He became an assistant professor, which is a professor without tenure, worked the required five to six years, and applied for tenure at the associate professor level. Three years later, he became a full professor.

Advice from a Professional. Although he was able to move directly into a tenure-track position with a master's degree, Marshall advises that today you will need a Ph.D. to achieve the same goal. "It's a wonderful thing to do if you get the chance to do it," he says. "You not only study and discuss interesting ideas, but you get to share them and watch them grow as you interact with young minds that aren't nearly as trained as yours but are flexible and hungry for the knowledge you have."

For Further Reading

Following are some examples of books that might be helpful as you pursue a career teaching in a college or university.

Bain, Ken. *What the Best College Teachers Do.* Cambridge, MA: Harvard University Press, 2004.

Filene, Peter. *The Joy of Teachers: A Practical Guide for New College Instructors.* Chapel Hill: University of North Carolina Press, 2005.

Fink, L. Dee. *Creating Significant Learning Experiences: An Integrated Approach to Designing College Courses.* San Francisco: Jossey-Bass, 2003.

A Final Thought

You now know what it takes to become a college instructor and have read the personal accounts of three professional teachers in different fields. If your love of research and sharing knowledge can't be denied, perhaps a career in the scholarly field of teaching is for you.

CHAPTER THREE

Librarians and Archivists

Librarians and archivists are excellent at research, one of the primary activities in which scholars indulge. Librarians make information available to people. They manage staff, oversee the collection and cataloging of materials, and develop and direct information programs for the public. They help users find information from printed materials and other resources.

Archivists handle collections that reflect the course of daily life for individuals and businesses. Some archives contain materials created by a specific institution. For example, years ago Coca Cola set up an archive to have a history of what the company business was and how it prospered. New companies establish archives to keep documented records. Other institutions, such as universities or museums, create archives that relate to their special research interests.

Nobody knows the exact number, but it's estimated that there are more than five thousand archives in the United States and Canada. Each of the fifty states maintains a government archives, as do most city and county governments. Archives are also found in historical societies, libraries, and private businesses. On the national level, the National Archives in Washington, D.C., looks after the records of the federal government. The Library of Congress provides information services to the U.S. Congress and technical services to all the libraries across the country. In Canada, each of the provinces maintains an archive, and Archives Canada provides links to each of those, as well as to municipal, university, religious, and medical archives.

Distinguishing Between Libraries and Archives

Although archives are similar to libraries, there are distinct differences between the two.

Libraries

Libraries typically house materials that are published and were created with the express purpose of broad dissemination. But the traditional concept of a library is being redefined from a place to access paper records or books to one that also houses the most advanced media, including CD-ROM, the Internet, virtual libraries, and remote access to a wide range of resources. Consequently, librarians, who are also called information professionals, increasingly are combining traditional duties with tasks involving quickly changing technology.

In order to assist people in finding information and using it effectively for personal and professional purposes, librarians must have knowledge of a wide variety of scholarly and public information sources. They must also follow trends related to publishing, computers, and the media in order to oversee the selection and organization of library materials. Librarians manage staff and develop and direct information programs and systems for the public to ensure that information is organized in a manner that meets users' needs.

Most librarian positions incorporate three aspects of library work:

- user services
- technical services
- administrative services

Librarians in user services, such as reference and children's librarians, work directly with users to help them find the information they need. This may involve analyzing users' needs to determine what information is appropriate and searching for, acquiring, and providing the information to users.

Those in technical services, such as acquisitions librarians and catalogers, acquire and prepare materials for use and may not deal directly with the public.

Administrative services librarians oversee the management of the library, supervising employees, preparing budgets, and directing activities to see that all parts of the library function properly. Their work also includes negotiating contracts for services, materials, and equipment; and performing public-relations and fundraising duties.

Depending on the work setting, librarians may perform a combination of user, technical, and administrative services. Still, even librarians specializing in one of these areas have other responsibilities. Librarians in user services often have an instructional role, such as showing users how to access information. For example, librarians commonly help users navigate the Internet so they can search for relevant information efficiently.

In small libraries or information centers, librarians usually handle all aspects of the work. They read book reviews, publishers' announcements, and catalogues to keep up with current literature and other available resources, and they select and purchase materials from publishers, wholesalers, and distributors. They prepare new materials by classifying them by subject matter and describing books and other library materials to make them easy to find. Librarians supervise assistants, who prepare cards, computer records, or other access tools that direct users to resources. Many working in large libraries specialize in a single area, such as acquisitions, cataloguing, bibliography, reference, special collections, or administration. Teamwork is increasingly important to ensure quality service to the public.

Librarians also compile lists of books, periodicals, articles, and audiovisual materials on particular subjects; analyze collections; and recommend materials. They collect and organize books, pamphlets, manuscripts, and other materials in a specific field, such as rare books, genealogy, or music. In addition, they coordinate programs such as storytelling for children and literacy skills and book talks for adults, conduct classes, publicize services, provide reference help, write grants, and oversee other administrative matters.

Librarians are also classified according to the type of library in which they work:

- public libraries
- school library media centers
- academic libraries
- specialty libraries

Some librarians work with specific groups, such as children, young adults, adults, or the disadvantaged. Those who work in school library media centers are often called school media specialists. They help teachers develop curricula, acquire materials for classroom instruction, and sometimes team teach.

Librarians also work in information centers or libraries maintained by government agencies, corporations, law firms, advertising agencies, museums, professional associations, unions, medical centers, hospitals, religious organizations, and research laboratories. They acquire and arrange an organization's information resources, which usually are limited to subjects of special interest to the organization. These special librarians can provide vital information services by preparing abstracts and indexes of current periodicals, organizing bibliographies, or analyzing background information and preparing reports on areas of particular interest.

For example, a special librarian working for a corporation could provide the sales department with information on competitors or new developments affecting the field. A medical librarian may provide information about new medical treatments, clinical trials, and standard procedures to health professionals, patients, consumers, and corporations. Government document librarians, who work for government agencies and depository libraries in each of the states and provinces, preserve government publications, records, and other documents that make up a historical record of government actions.

Many libraries have access to remote databases and maintain their own computerized databases. The widespread use of automation in libraries makes database-searching skills important to librarians, who develop and index databases and help users learn the skills required to search for the information they need. Some libraries are forming consortia to allow patrons to access a wider range of databases and to submit information requests to several libraries simultaneously. The Internet also has greatly expanded the amount of available reference information, and librarians must be aware of how to use these resources in order to locate information.

More and more, librarians are applying their information management and research skills to arenas outside of libraries, such as database development, reference tool development, information systems, publishing, Internet coordination, marketing, Web content management and design, and training of database users.

Librarians with computer and information systems skills can work as automated-systems librarians, planning and operating computer systems, and as information architects, designing information storage and retrieval systems and developing procedures for collecting, organizing, interpreting, and classifying information. These librarians analyze and plan for future needs. The increasing use of automated systems is enabling librarians to focus on administrative and budgeting responsibilities, grant writing, and specialized research requests while delegating more technical and user services responsibilities to technicians.

About two out of ten librarians work part-time. Public and college librarians often work weekends and evenings, as well as some holidays. School librarians usually have the same workday and vacation schedules as classroom teachers. Special librarians usually work normal business hours, but in fast-paced industries, such as advertising or legal services, they can work longer hours when needed. Entrepreneurial librarians sometimes start their own consulting practices, acting as freelance librarians or information brokers and providing services to libraries, businesses, or government agencies.

Archives

Archives typically hold materials that were created in the course of carrying out some sort of business or activity but that were never originally intended for public dissemination. For example, an archive might hold correspondence from a Civil War soldier to his family. He wrote about his experiences and feelings and to let his loved ones know that he was still alive. Although he never would have imagined that his letters would one day appear in an archives, their inclusion provides credibility and integrity as a historical source.

Archivists collect, organize, and maintain control over a wide range of information deemed important enough for permanent safekeeping. This information takes many forms: photographs, films, video and sound recordings, computer disks or tapes, and video and optical disks, as well as more traditional paper records, letters, and documents. Archivists work for a variety of organizations, including government agencies, museums, historical societies, corporations, and educational institutions—any organization that uses or generates records of great potential value to researchers, exhibitors, genealogists, and others who would benefit from having access to original source material.

These scholars maintain records in accordance with accepted standards and practices that ensure the long-term preservation and easy retrieval of the documents. Records may be saved on any medium, including paper, film, videotape, audiotape, electronic disk, or computer. They also may be copied onto some other format to protect the original and to make the records more accessible to researchers who use them. As various storage media evolve, archivists must keep abreast of technological advances in electronic information storage.

Archivists often specialize in an area of history or technology so they can more accurately determine which records in that area qualify for retention and should become part of the archives. They also may work with specialized forms of records, such as manuscripts, electronic records, photographs, cartographic records, motion pictures, and sound recordings.

As computers are increasingly being used to generate and maintain archival records, professional standards for the use of computers in handling archival records are still evolving. Expanding computer capabilities that allow more records to be stored and exhibited electronically have transformed, and are expected to continue to transform, many aspects of archival collections.

Some archivists spend most of their time working with the public, providing reference assistance and educational services. Others perform research or process records, which often means working alone or in offices with only a few people.

Training

Now that you know the differences between libraries and archives, let's see what qualifications and training you'll need for both of these challenging jobs.

Librarians

You'll need a master's degree in library science (M.L.S.) for librarian positions in most public, academic, and special libraries and in some school libraries. To work for the federal government, you will need an M.L.S. or the equivalent in education and experience. While you can find M.L.S. programs at many colleges and universities, a number of employers prefer graduates of the approximately fifty-six schools in North America that are accredited by the American Library Association.

Most M.L.S. programs take one year to complete; some take two. There is no specific undergraduate major required. In a typical graduate program, your courses will cover the foundations of library and information science, including the history of books and printing, intellectual freedom and censorship, and the role of libraries and information in society. You'll also study the selection and processing of materials, the organization of information, reference tools and strategies, and user services.

Courses are adapted to educate librarians to use new resources brought about by advancing technology, such as online reference systems, Internet search methods, and automated circulation systems. Your course options can include resources for children or young adults; classification, cataloguing, indexing, and abstracting; library administration; and library automation. Computer-related course work is an increasingly important part of an M.L.S. degree. Some programs allow you to earn an interdisciplinary degree combining technical courses in information science with traditional training in library science.

While an M.L.S. degree provides general preparation for library work, you may wish to specialize in a particular area, such as reference, technical services, or children's services. A Ph.D. in library and information science is advantageous for a college teaching position or for a top administrative job in a college or university library or large library system.

In addition to an M.L.S. degree, most special librarians supplement their education with knowledge of the field in which they are specializing, sometimes earning a master's, doctoral, or professional degree in the subject. Areas of specialization include medicine, law, business, engineering, and the natural and social sciences. For example, a librarian working for a law firm may also be a licensed attorney, holding both library science and law degrees, while medical librarians should have a strong background in the sciences. Some jobs also require knowledge of a foreign language.

Most states and provinces have certification requirements for librarians in public schools and local libraries, but the requirements vary by jurisdiction. Many require school librarians to be certified as teachers in addition to taking courses in library science. Some require an M.L.S., often with a library media specialization, while in others a master's in education with a specialty in school library media or educational media is needed. Be sure to find out whether your state or province requires certification of librarians employed in local library systems.

Librarians participate in continuing education and training in order to keep abreast of new information systems brought about by changing technology. Experienced librarians can advance to administrative positions, such as department head, library director, or chief information officer.

Archivists

To work as an archivist, you will need a graduate degree and related work experience—perhaps gained working in an archive while completing your formal education. Although archivists earn a variety of undergraduate degrees, most employers prefer a graduate degree in history or library science, with courses in archival science. You may find that some positions require knowledge of the discipline related to the collection, such as business or medicine.

A few institutions now offer master's degrees in archival studies. Many colleges and universities offer courses or practical training in archival science as part of their history, library science, or other curriculum. The Academy of Certified Archivists offers voluntary certification for archivists. You are eligible for the designation Certified Archivist once you have completed your master's degree and a year of appropriate archival experience. The certification process requires that you pass a written examination, and you must renew your certification periodically.

Archivists need research and analytical ability to understand the content of documents and the context in which they were created and to decipher deteriorated or poor-quality printed matter, handwritten manuscripts, photographs, or films. A background in preservation management is often required because archivists are responsible for taking proper care of their records.

They also must be able to organize large amounts of information and write clear instructions for its retrieval and use. In addition, computer skills and the ability to work with electronic records and databases are very important. Because electronic records are becoming the prevalent form of record keeping and archivists must be able to create searchable databases, a knowledge of Web technology is increasingly required.

Many archives, including one-person shops, are very small and have limited opportunities for promotion. In these settings, archivists typically advance by transferring to a larger unit that has supervisory positions. A doctorate in history, library science, or a related field may be needed for some advanced positions, such as director of a state or provincial archive.

Continuing education, which enables archivists to keep up with developments in the field, is available through meetings, conferences, and workshops sponsored by archival associations. Some larger organizations, such as the National Archives, offer in-house training.

Job Outlook

Although employment of librarians is expected to grow only as much as 8 percent through 2014, job opportunities are expected to be good because a large number of librarians are expected to retire in the coming decade. More than three in five librarians are aged forty-five or older and will become eligible for retirement in the next ten years, which will result in numerous job openings. Also, the number of people going into this profession has fallen in recent years, resulting in more jobs than applicants in some cases.

Growth in the number of librarians will be limited by government budget constraints and the increasing use of computerized information storage and retrieval systems. Both will result in the hiring of fewer librarians and the replacement of some with less costly library technicians and assistants. Computerized systems make cataloguing easier, allowing library technicians to perform the work. In addition, many libraries are equipped for users to access library computers directly from their homes or offices, allowing them to bypass librarians altogether and conduct research on their own. However, librarians will still be needed to manage staff, help users develop database-searching techniques, address complicated reference requests, and define users' needs.

Jobs for librarians outside traditional settings are expected to show the fastest growth. Nontraditional librarian jobs include working as information brokers and working for private corporations, nonprofit organizations, and consulting firms. Many companies are turning to librarians because of their research and organizational skills and their knowledge of computer databases and library automation systems. Librarians can review vast amounts of information and analyze, evaluate, and organize it according to a company's specific needs. They are also hired by organizations to set up information on the Internet. Those working in these settings may be classified as systems analysts, database specialists and trainers, Web developers, or local area network (LAN) coordinators.

Archivists can expect keen competition for positions because qualified applicants generally outnumber job openings. Graduates with highly specialized training, such as master's degrees in both library science and history, with a concentration in archives or records management and extensive computer skills, should have the best opportunities.

Employment of archivists is expected to grow between 9 and 17 percent through 2014, as information increases and public and private organizations emphasize establishing archives and organizing records. Additional demand will be generated by strong public and private support for and interest in museums. However, museums and other cultural institutions can be subject to cuts in funding during recessions or periods of budget tightening, reducing demand for these workers. Although the rate of turnover among archivists is relatively low, the need to replace workers who leave the occupation or stop working will create some additional job openings.

Salaries

Salaries of librarians vary according to individual qualifications and the type, size, and location of the library. Librarians with primarily administrative duties often have greater earnings.

Median annual earnings of librarians in 2004 were $45,900. The majority earned between $36,980 and $56,960, while the lowest 10 percent earned less than $28,930, and the highest 10 percent earned more than $70,200.

The average annual salary for all librarians in the federal government was $74,630 in 2005.

Median annual earnings in the industries that employ the largest numbers of librarians are as follows:

Colleges, universities, and professional schools	$47,830
Elementary and secondary schools	$47,580
Local government	$42,500
Other information services	$40,000

About three in ten librarians are members of a union or are covered under a union contract.

Median annual earnings of archivists in 2004 were $36,470. Most earned between $28,900 and $46,480. The lowest 10 percent earned less than $21,780, and the highest 10 percent earned more than $61,260.

In 2005, the average annual salary for archivists in the federal government was $75,876.

. . . .

Profiles

Two librarians and an archivist have shared their stories with us. Read their accounts to learn more about these fields.

Steve Oserman—Reference Librarian

Steve Oserman generously shared his personal account for this book. Sadly, he has since passed away, but his contribution about the career that he loved is still a valuable addition to this chapter.

Steve worked as a reference librarian in the Adult Services Department with the Skokie Public Library in Illinois. He had more than thirty years of combined teaching and library experience. He coauthored *The Guide to Internet Job Searching* with Margaret Riley and Frances Roehm, and he developed two books through the Job and Career Information Services Committee of the Public Library Association called *The Basic Guide to Resume Writing* and *The Basic Guide to Cover Letter Writing*.

The day was structured so that Steve worked on the reference desk for two hours, and then he was off for two hours. While at the desk, he helped people with general reference questions on a variety of topics and assisted patrons with the Internet and CD-ROMs. Off the desk, he ran the library's employment resource center, helping patrons with resumes, job changes, and Internet job search strategies.

He also served as cochair of job and career information services for the Public Library Association, a position that allowed him to speak nationally and to train librarians to develop their expertise in helping people find jobs and start career centers.

Steve also led book discussions and presented many lectures and programs. Most involved Internet job searching, but he also gave presentations on such diverse topics as dreams, health, and healing for area hospitals. He also traded options and gave lectures on technical analysis of stock option trends. In addition, he did Chinese astrology and *I Ching*. "I always tell people to pursue at least seven careers simultaneously," Steve said. "I'm trying to have at least fourteen.

"I like my work a lot," he continued, "but I don't like meetings and the bureaucratic paperwork. I like things that involve people. I'm very extroverted, and I like helping people find jobs or motivation. And I enjoy the seminars and public speaking I do."

He officially worked thirty-seven and a half hours a week, but he spent a lot more time than that on the job. He generally came in early, and he also worked in the evenings, doing his committee work on his days off.

Getting Started. Steve earned a B.S. in mathematics and philosophy from the University of Illinois at Champaign-Urbana and completed substantial work toward a Ph.D. in philosophy at Southern Illinois University at Carbondale, where he also taught philosophy.

He explained that his situation was atypical because he never attended library school. He started his career at a time when there was a shortage of librarians and got his training on the job. And because he had more than two hundred credits of graduate work in other fields, his employers considered that comparable to at least one year of library school.

Steve explained that he initially started in library work as a way to help finance his college education, rather than actively pursuing it as a career. Although he was unhappy in the early years when he was doing more traditional librarian work, he found his niche when he became more involved with career information areas, which made the work much more interesting to him.

Advice from a Professional. "This career is not just being around books; it's really being around people much more," Steve explained. "A lot of people think they might be a good candidate for a library job just because they like to be around books, but, actually, that's exactly what's not needed. There is probably a too high percentage of introverted people who are already in the library profession, as compared to the general population. We need more extroverted people."

He found that many of the people working in libraries love their work. Through his seminars, he met many librarians who truly enjoy their jobs but who would like to have more career development possibilities. He said that a librarian may plateau when there is not enough room for advancement, which should be taken into consideration when choosing this career.

Carol Jones—Technical Services Librarian

Carol Jones works at the Kline Science Library, one of many libraries at Yale University in New Haven, Connecticut. She has been a librarian for more than twenty years.

Technical services is a broad term that includes acquisitions and the cataloging and binding of materials. Carol explains that her position is very similar to working in a business; in her case, acquisitions means buying materials—books and electronic resources. The latter includes the many journals that are available in electronic format over the Internet, as opposed to being printed in hard-copy format.

The library's budget for acquisitions is over $1 million, making this big business. Once materials are ordered, the staff has to see that they're received and made available on the shelves. Since Carol's position is administrative, she supervises four people, monitors budgets, writes policies and procedures, and trains staff. She also meets with vendors, works on problems, and serves on committees in the university library that work with a wide range of issues.

She also spends a good deal of time working with computers. The library has a local area network, with work stations for all staff members and for patrons. In addition to her own work, Carol coordinates the computer work for the five other science libraries at Yale.

"I like the detail of it and the business orientation of it," she says. "I never really wanted to go into the corporate world. Academe does have nice benefits in terms of vacation time and a certain flexibility I think would be missing in a corporate setting.

"From what I've heard from friends who work in public libraries, I think I'd much prefer the university setting I'm in. The patrons are very different. The public libraries deal with current readings; they have children and adults with a real wide range of interests. We have students and faculty who are fairly focused."

The job does include a considerable amount of pressure and stress, however, most of which comes from an increasing emphasis on downsizing, resource reallocation, and greater productivity with fewer people. In addition, rapidly changing technology makes it difficult to keep up with current advances.

Getting Started. Carol earned her B.A. in history from Kentucky Wesleyan and her M.L.S. from the University of Kentucky in Lexington in the School of Library and Information Science. She worked for nine years at the library at Kentucky Wesleyan, then went to Yale as a government documents librarian.

Her interest in library work began when she was an undergraduate. Carol started college later than most undergraduates, when she was already married and had three children. Her interest stemmed mainly from her own use of the library, but she didn't pursue it until her last year of college, when she began working part-time in the library.

Part of her desire to work in a library was a love of books combined with an interest in publishing, information, and research. She also took some undergraduate classes in library science and found cataloging and organizing materials very interesting.

Also, on a practical level, working in a library offered Carol the opportunity for a career with flexibility, which was important because she had young children. She decided to get a master's degree because she knew that was the only way to earn an acceptable salary.

Advice from a Professional. Carol feels that the increased availability of electronic resources will make the field of librarianship even more interesting and important. As information expands at an ever faster rate, librarians will be integral in making that information understandable and accessible to the people who need it. "It's one thing to say everyone will have a computer and they'll be able to do it all themselves," she says. "But in actuality, someone who is familiar with the way the information is organized and how you can get at it is going to be crucial. And that someone is going to be a librarian. Knowledge of computers and information resources is absolutely essential. Subject expertise and language expertise has always been useful, too, and it will be even more so in the future."

John Fleckner—Chief Archivist

John Fleckner came to the National Museum of American History at the Smithsonian Institution in 1982 with more than a decade's experience working as an archivist for the State Historical Society of Wisconsin. He is a past president of the Society of American Archivists and has acted as a consultant on many important archives projects, including the United Negro College Fund, the Vietnam History and Archives Project, and the Native American Archives Project.

"Archivists provide a service to society by identifying and preserving materials with lasting value for the future," he explains. "When archivists talk about their work, they discuss certain basic functions that are common to all archives."

John oversees a professional staff of twelve archivists, three student interns, and close to twenty volunteers. About 50 percent of his time is spent in supervision, and the rest covers identifying and acquiring materials, providing reference services, and handling administrative duties, such as meetings, budget, and personnel. He is also involved in outreach and public affairs.

The archives he is responsible for acquires collections from the outside and does not handle the records generated by the museum. The collections cover a wide range of subjects and are particularly strong in the areas of American music, advertising, and the history of technology. He explains that, while each item in a library is a distinct entity evaluated separately from the others, in an archives, a single letter would usually be part of a larger collection of letters. Archivists are interested in these as a group because one letter would only be a fragment. To really understand something about the past, the information needs to be synthesized and put together to form a collection.

Getting Started. John graduated from Colgate University in Hamilton, New York, earning a B.A. with honors in history. He earned his M.A. in American history at the University of Wisconsin and also has completed significant work toward his Ph.D.

He attended graduate school with the idea of teaching college-level history, but he realized that he really didn't want to teach. "I was so naive," he says, "it took a university career counselor to recognize that my history background might be anything other than an economic liability."

The counselor suggested that John look into a recently established graduate program in archives administration at the State Historical Society of Wisconsin. The program instructor would make no promises about the prospects for a job but did offer that all his previous students were working.

Once he began doing archival work, beginning with the simplest class exercises and then a formal internship, John was hooked. He loved the combination of handicraft and analytical work, as well as the intense, intimate contact with the stuff of history. Before he completed his internship, he knew that he wanted to be an archivist.

He had done some research in archives as a graduate student, but he felt that the materials were antiseptically stored, boxed, and listed. He says, "Wheeled out on carts, they were like cadavers to be dissected by first-year medical students. On occasion, I even donned white gloves. The documents always seemed lifeless.

"Later, as a would-be archivist, they thrilled me. I was in charge; I would evaluate the significance of the materials, determine their order, describe their contents, and physically prepare them for their permanent resting places. Still, it was not so much this heady feeling of control that awed me as it was the mystery, the possibilities of the records themselves. My judgments would be critical to building paths to the records for generations of researchers, across the entire spectrum of topics, and into unknown future time."

Working as an archivist holds another attraction for John. In addition to the opportunity to reconstruct the past captured in the documents and to imagine the future research they might support, he has a well-defined task to accomplish. He enjoys having a product to produce, techniques and methods for proceeding, and standards against which his work is judged. The rigor and discipline of the work appeals to him, and he thoroughly enjoys his job.

Advice from a Professional. People get into the archives profession in a variety of traditional and unusual ways. Often in a small town, an archive is a closet in the back room of a local historical society's office. Someone volunteers to put it all together and thus becomes the town's archivist. But if you want to work in a professional, paid position, John recommends that you pursue either a degree in history with specific archives courses or a master's degree in library science with courses in archives administration.

For Further Reading

You may find some useful information in the following books, which are an example of the resources available for planning your career.

Bell, Suzanne S. *Librarian's Guide to Online Searching*. Westport, CT: Libraries Unlimited, 2006.

Cassell, Kay Ann, and Uma Hiremath. *Reference and Information Services in the 21st Century: An Introduction*. New York: Neal-Schuman Publishers, 2006.

Cox, Richard J. *Archives and Archivists in the Information Age*. New York: Neal-Schuman Publishers, 2005.

Shepherd, Elizabeth. *Management Skills for Archivists and Records Managers*. London: Facet Publishing, 2008.

Taylor, Arlene G. *Introduction to Cataloging and Classification*, 10th ed. Westport, CT: Libraries Unlimited, 2006.

A Final Thought

This chapter has introduced you to librarians and archivists, scholars whose love of organizing information resources and helping others to use them led them to challenging careers. These professions are well-suited to scholarly types who have the right combination of research skills and personal attributes to pursue the necessary training.

CHAPTER FOUR

Social Scientists

ocial scientists study all aspects of human society, from past events and achievements to human behavior and relationships among groups. Their research provides insights that help us understand the different ways in which individuals and groups make decisions, exercise power, or respond to change. Through their studies and analyses, social scientists assist educators, government officials, business leaders, and others in solving social, economic, and environmental problems.

Research is one of the primary activities of many social scientists, who use established or newly developed methods to assemble facts and theories that contribute to human knowledge. Applied research is usually designed to produce information that will enable people to make better decisions or manage their lives more effectively. Interviews and surveys are used to collect facts, opinions, or other information. Data collection takes many other forms, however, including living and working among the people studied; archaeological and other field investigations; analyzing historical records and documents; experimenting with human subjects or animals in a psychological laboratory; administering standardized tests and questionnaires; and preparing and interpreting maps and graphic materials.

Social Science Disciplines

Because social sciences are interdisciplinary in nature, the research conducted by specialists in one field often overlaps work that is being conducted in another discipline. Regardless of their fields of specialization, social scientists are concerned with some aspect of society, culture, or personality.

- **Anthropologists** study the origin and the physical, social, and cultural development and behavior of humans. They may study the way of life, remains, language, or physical characteristics of people in various parts of the world, comparing customs, values, and social patterns of different cultures. Anthropologists generally concentrate in socio-cultural anthropology, archaeology, biological-physical anthropology, or linguistics. Sociocultural anthropologists study the customs, cultures, and social lives of groups in a wide range of settings, from nonindustrialized societies to modern urban cultures. Linguistic anthropologists study the role of language in various cultures. Biological-physical anthropologists study the evolution of the human body and look for the earliest evidences of human life.
- **Archaeologists** are part of a subdivision of anthropology. Archaeologists study the artifacts of past cultures to learn about their histories, customs, and living habits. They survey and excavate archaeological sites, recording and cataloging their finds, and reconstruct earlier cultures and determine their influences on the present. (See Chapter 5 for more on archaeologists.)
- **Economists** study the production, distribution, and consumption of commodities and services. They may conduct surveys and analyze data to determine public preferences for these goods and services. Most economists are concerned with the practical applications of economic policy in a particular area, such as finance, labor, agriculture, transportation, energy, or health. Others develop theories to explain economic phenomena such as unemployment or inflation. Marketing research analysts research market conditions in localities, regions, the nation, or the world to determine

potential sales of a product or service; they examine and analyze data on past sales and trends to develop forecasts.

- **Geographers** study the distribution of both physical and cultural phenomena on local, regional, continental, and global scales. Most specialize in a particular field. Economic geographers study the regional distribution of resources and economic activities. Political geographers are concerned with the relationship of geography to political phenomena at local, national, and international levels. Physical geographers study the distribution of climates, vegetation, soil, and land forms. Urban and transportation geographers study cities and metropolitan areas, while regional geographers study the physical, climatic, economic, political, and cultural characteristics of regions, ranging in size from a congressional district to a state, country, continent, or the entire world. Medical geographers study health care delivery systems, epidemiology, and the effect of the environment on health. Geographic Information Systems (GIS) analysts work in a geographic specialty that combines computer graphics, artificial intelligence, and high-speed communication to store, retrieve, manipulate, analyze, and map geographic data. GIS is widely used in weather forecasting, emergency management, and resource analysis and management.

- **Historians** research and analyze the past. They use many information sources in their research, including government and institutional records, newspapers and other periodicals, photographs, interviews, films, and unpublished manuscripts such as diaries and letters. Historians usually specialize in a specific country or region; in a particular time period; or in a particular field, such as social, intellectual, political, or diplomatic history. Biographers collect detailed information on individuals. Genealogists trace family histories. Other historians help study and preserve archival materials, artifacts, and historic buildings and sites. (See Chapters 3 and 7 for close-ups of an archivist and a history museum curator and Chapter 10 for more about genealogists.)

- **Political scientists** study the origin, development, and operation of political systems. They conduct research on a wide range of subjects, such as relations between the United States and foreign countries, the beliefs and institutions of foreign nations (for example, those in Asia and Africa), the politics of small towns or a major metropolis, or the decisions of the U.S. Supreme Court. Studying topics such as public opinion, political decision making, and ideology, they analyze the structure and operation of governments as well as informal political entities. Depending on the topic, a political scientist might conduct a public opinion survey, analyze election results, or analyze public documents.

- **Psychologists**, who comprise more than half of all social scientists, study human behavior and counsel or advise individuals or groups. Their research also assists business advertisers, politicians, and others interested in influencing or motivating people. While clinical psychology is the largest specialty, psychologists focus on many other fields, such as counseling, experimental, social, or industrial psychology. (See Chapter 6 for a more detailed look at the psychology profession.)

- **Sociologists** analyze the development, structure, and behavior of groups or social systems such as families, neighborhoods, or clubs. They may specialize in a particular field, such as criminology, rural sociology, or medical sociology.

- **Urban and regional planners** develop comprehensive plans and programs for the use of land for industrial and public sites. Planners prepare for situations that are likely to develop as a result of population growth or social and economic change.

Working Conditions

Most social scientists have regular hours. They generally work in offices, both alone and in collaboration with other social scientists, reading and writing research reports. Many work as an integral part of a research team. They often face deadlines and tight schedules, and sometimes they must work overtime, for which they generally are not reimbursed.

Travel may be necessary to collect information or attend meetings, and those working on foreign assignments must adjust to unfamiliar cultures and climates.

Some social scientists do fieldwork. For example, anthropologists, archaeologists, and geographers often must travel to remote areas, live among the people they study, and stay for long periods at the site of their investigations. They may work under primitive conditions, and their work may involve strenuous physical exertion.

Those employed by colleges and universities usually have flexible work schedules, often dividing their time among teaching, research, consulting, or administrative responsibilities.

Employment Options

Social scientists hold about 450,000 jobs throughout North America. Many work as researchers, administrators, and counselors for a wide range of employers, and about half work for federal, state, provincial, and local governments, mostly in the federal government. Other employers include scientific research and development services; management, scientific, and technical consulting services; business, professional, labor, political, and similar organizations; and architectural, engineering, and related firms.

In addition, many people with training in a social science discipline teach in colleges and universities (see Chapter 2) and in secondary and elementary schools. The proportion of social scientists who teach varies by occupation. For example, the academic world generally is a more important source of jobs for graduates in sociology than for graduates in psychology.

Training

If you choose to work in social science, you will be among the most highly educated group of professionals among all occupations. A Ph.D. or an equivalent degree is the minimum requirement for most positions in colleges and universities and is important for advancement to many top-level nonacademic research and administrative posts.

A master's degree in an applied specialty will prepare you for opportunities outside of colleges and universities, although the situation varies by field. You may also be qualified to teach in a community college.

You'll have limited opportunities with a bachelor's degree in most social science occupations, and you will not be qualified for professional positions. You will, however, be qualified for many different entry-level jobs, such as research assistant, administrative aide, or management or sales trainee. With additional education courses, you can also qualify for teaching positions in secondary and elementary schools.

To work in certain fields of social science, you may need training in statistics and mathematics. For example, quantitative research methods are increasingly used in geography, political science, sociology, and other fields. The ability to utilize computers for research purposes is mandatory in most disciplines. Most geographers, and increasing numbers of archaeologists, also need to be familiar with GIS technology.

You may find that an internship or field experience will be beneficial in establishing yourself in one of the social sciences. Check with local museums, historical societies, government agencies, and other organizations for internships or volunteer research opportunities.

Depending on the field you choose, you may need a wide range of personal characteristics. Intellectual curiosity and creativity are fundamental because social scientists constantly seek new information about people, things, and ideas. The ability to think logically and methodically is important to a political scientist comparing, for example, the merits of various forms of government. Objectivity, an open mind, and systematic work habits are important in all kinds of social science research. Perseverance is essential for an anthropologist, who might have to spend years studying artifacts from an ancient civilization before making a final analysis and interpretation. Excellent written and oral communication skills also are necessary for all of these professionals.

Job Outlook

Although overall employment of social scientists is expected to grow only as much as eight percent through 2014, projected growth rates vary by specialty. Anthropologists should experience average employment growth, while employment of geographers, historians, political scientists, and sociologists will grow more slowly, mainly because fewer opportunities exist outside of government and academic settings. Job growth will be very slow in the federal government, a key employer of social scientists.

Anthropologists should see the majority of their employment growth in the management, scientific, and technical consulting services industry. Anthropologists who work as consultants often apply anthropological knowledge and methods to problems ranging from economic development issues to forensics.

Competition will be keen for social science positions. Many jobs in policy, research, or marketing for which social scientists qualify are not advertised exclusively as social scientist positions.

Because of their wide range of skills and knowledge, many social scientists compete for jobs with other workers, such as market and survey researchers, engineers, and statisticians.

A few social scientists will find opportunities as university faculty, although competition for these jobs also will remain strong. Usually, there are more graduates than available faculty positions, although retirements among faculty are expected to rise in the next few years. The growing importance and popularity of social science subjects in secondary schools is strengthening the demand for social science teachers at that level.

Geographers will have opportunities to utilize their skills to advise government, real estate developers, utilities, and telecommunications firms on where to construct new roads, buildings, and power plants and install cable lines. They will also advise on environmental matters, such as where to build a landfill or preserve wetland habitats. Geographers with a background in GIS will find many opportunities applying this technology in nontraditional areas, such as emergency assistance, where GIS can track locations of ambulances, police, and fire rescue units and their proximity to the emergency. Workers in these jobs may be referred to by a different title, such as GIS analyst or GIS specialist. GIS technology also will be utilized in areas of growing importance, such as homeland security and defense.

Historians, political scientists, and sociologists will find jobs in policy or research. Historians may find opportunities with historic preservation societies as public interest in preserving and restoring historical sites increases. Political scientists will be able to utilize their knowledge of political institutions to further the interests of nonprofit, political, and social organizations. Sociologists may find work conducting policy research for consulting firms and nonprofit organizations, and their knowledge of society and social behavior may be used by a variety of companies in product development, marketing, and advertising.

Salaries

In 2004, anthropologists had median annual earnings of $43,890; geographers, $58,970; historians, $44,490; political scientists, $86,750; and sociologists, $57,870.

In 2005 in the federal government, social scientists with a bachelor's degree and no experience could start at a yearly salary between $24,677 and $30,567, depending on their college records. Those with a master's degree could start at $37,390; those with a doctoral degree could begin at $45,239, while some individuals with experience and an advanced degree could start at $54,221. Beginning salaries were slightly higher in selected areas of the country where the prevailing local pay level was higher.

Profile

Read this interesting account from a social scientist—does it pique your interest?

Ann Gardner—Social Anthropologist

Ann Gardner is a social anthropologist who has done extensive fieldwork in the Middle East, especially working with Bedouin women in the Sinai Desert. She earned her B.A. in anthropology from Friends World College (Jerusalem Center) and studied Arabic for two years at the American University in Cairo. She received both her M.A. and Ph.D. in anthropology from the University of Texas at Austin.

All of her education, and over six years of living in the Middle East, resulted in a doctoral dissertation titled "Women and Changing Relations in a South Sinai Bedouin Community."

Getting Started. Ann believes that she has always been interested in other places and even named a childhood toy "Journey" because she planned to bring it on all of her travels. She thinks that the inspiration came from the nightly bedtime stories her mother read to her, combined with her own natural interests.

She took some anthropology courses in high school and majored in anthropology in college. Since she attended a college with centers around the world that stressed cross-cultural experience, she had far more field experience than most graduate students.

Ann explains that most large university anthropology graduate departments offer programs in social-cultural anthropology, economic anthropology, physical anthropology, linguistics, folklore, archaeology, museum studies, and, sometimes, development anthropology. Some of these specializations overlap to certain degrees, and the professors have expertise in various geographical regions. Students may also take classes from other departments.

She recommends choosing your area of specialization before entering graduate school to study anthropology. As a graduate student, you will be required to take core classes covering the various specializations, but generally the more undergraduate courses you've completed in your area of interest, the better your chances are of getting into graduate school. Most students also already know which world regions they are interested in, too.

Based on her own education experience, Ann says that you need to have, or quickly learn, many skills to be a successful anthropology graduate student. You should be able to perform very well academically, which usually means not taking incompletes and not getting more than one B. In her own studies, students were expected to read around five hundred pages a week, per class. Most full-time graduate students took three courses a semester, while some took four.

You need to be able to write theoretically for an academic audience and also still be able to write well for the general public, and grant-writing skills are a must for gaining the support needed to conduct research. If you are working as a teaching assistant, you'll likely need course-development and teaching skills. In this capacity, you'll also need rapid grading skills, because you will often have several hundred exams and essays to read at once, usually at the same time that your own papers and exams are due. You need to be able to do research, which, for anthropologists, often includes living in another culture while doing cross-cultural fieldwork.

Anthropology is a diversified field, which has the potential to grow with your evolving interests. As an undergraduate social anthropology student researching Sinai Bedouin women, Ann's initial attraction to the field was her interest in other cultures and in promoting international understanding. Over the years, she saw the Bedouins become increasingly marginalized by development, and she became interested in that subfield as well, since anthropologists are in a good position to help voice the concerns of people and help access the possibilities for change.

Advice from a Professional. If you are interested in majoring in anthropology as an undergraduate, Ann strongly recommends that you attend a good college that offers anthropology, rather than a large university where you will likely get little personal attention.

If you are interested in working in anthropology, you will need to go on to graduate school. Ann explains that graduate training in anthropology is an enormous commitment, in terms of both time and money. Ten years is about the average for getting an M.A. and Ph.D., and you must also face the financial reality of undertaking graduate school.

Ann was fortunate to have been offered teaching assistantships from her first semester, and she also received numerous grants as well as the support of her parents. This doesn't always happen, however, and many students must work outside of the school and must repay student loans after graduation.

She also stresses the importance of taking fellowship and grant writing classes early on, since most anthropologists need this vital skill to do funded field research and writing. Ann has received funding from the National Science Foundation, the Wenner-Gren Anthropological Society, the American Research Center in Egypt, and the Research and Exploration Committee of the National Geographic Society.

Ann suggests that you choose your graduate school, subspecialization, and potential graduate advisor very carefully. The main focus in your graduate program will be academics, unless you select an applied program or have previous in-depth field experience to draw on. Many programs focus on training students in postmodern theory and teaching. Some also offer museum and folklore studies and may include training for museum positions, which you may be able to get with an M.A.

She reinforces that the competition is very steep for teaching positions and that you will need a Ph.D. for a professorship or even a lecturer position. In light of this, she suggests that you may be more marketable if you can teach in more than one discipline. For example, an anthropologist might get a job as a women's studies or religious studies professor. It isn't uncommon to find hundreds of applicants for an open position, even for one with a low starting salary. Some Ph.D.s take jobs as teachers in private high schools, which can be easier to secure and may pay more.

If your interest is in applied anthropology and you want a full-time job at a development, government, or nongovernment agency, you should also take management courses and secure intern positions with an agency. Although a Ph.D. is best, some positions can be obtained with an M.A.

Other applied anthropologists do contract research. While this can be unreliable, it is becoming more common for development agencies, for example, to want the input of anthropologists. Ann focused on development as one of her specializations, and, even before she'd completed her Ph.D., was offered the possibility of working on a three-year Bedouin-related development project. Her first priority at the time, however, was to rewrite her dissertation into a book for popular press publication. Most people publish their dissertations with an academic press, but Ann wanted to reach a wide audience, including students, academics, development personnel, and the general public.

As a practicing anthropologist, Ann is continuing her interest in writing and field research. She receives income from professional writing, grants, and consulting contract work for development agencies, research organizations, and similar organizations. She also may teach at some point, although she is not interested in being a full-time professor.

For Further Reading

The following titles are just a few representative examples of the many books available in the various areas of the social sciences.

Ferraro, Gary. *Classic Readings in Cultural Anthropology*. Boston: Wadsworth Publishing, 2003.

Gould, Peter. *Becoming a Geographer*. Syracuse: Syracuse University Press, 2000.

Omohundro, John. *Thinking Like an Anthropologist: A Practical Introduction to Cultural Anthropology*. New York: McGraw-Hill, 2007.

Samuelson, Paul A., and William A. Barnett, Eds. *Inside the Economist's Mind: Conversations with Eminent Economists*. New York: Wiley, 2006.

A Final Thought

The social sciences provide many opportunities for scholars to use their skills in a variety of exciting careers. From interviewing people about their customs and habits to studying political systems or planning land use, this broad area gives you plenty of options to consider for your future.

CHAPTER FIVE

Archaeologists

A rchaeologists study the artifacts of past cultures to learn about their histories, customs, and living habits. They survey and excavate archaeological sites, recording and cataloging their finds, and reconstruct earlier cultures and determine their influences on the present.

Archaeological sites are the physical remains of past civilizations. They can include building debris and the items found inside, in addition to trash and garbage. Usually these sites have been buried by other, later human activity or by natural processes, making excavation a painstaking process conducted by professionals using modern techniques. Because these sites are so fragile, the very nature of excavating destroys some information. With this in mind, archaeologists are careful to dig only as much as they need to answer important questions. Frequently, archaeologists concentrate their work on sites slated to be destroyed for highway or new building construction.

Working Conditions

Archaeologists work in a variety of settings. Archaeologists conducting fieldwork often work with several other professionals in a team effort. They are assisted by geologists, ethnologists, educators, anthropologists, ecologists, and aerial photographers.

In the field, archaeologists use a variety of tools during an excavation. These include picks, shovels, trowels, wheelbarrows, sifting boxes, pressure sprayers, and brushes. Archaeologists also make on-site drawings and sketches and take notes and photographs.

The following chart lists the various settings in which archaeologists work and the duties specific to each.

SETTINGS	DUTIES	WORK SETTINGS
Universities and colleges	teaching, fieldwork, research, directing student fieldwork	classrooms, labs, offices
Private institutions and museums	fieldwork, research, classifying, preserving, displaying	display and research areas, offices
Public sector (local, state, and national government agencies)	excavating, surveying, analyzing, preserving, recording	field sites, labs, research facilities
Private sector (construction companies, architectural firms)	excavating, surveying, preserving, recording	field sites, labs, research facilities

Qualifications

Do you have what it takes to become an archaeologist? Take this self-evaluation quiz to find out. Answer true or false to the following statements.

1. I have above-average academic ability.
2. I have an avid interest in science and history.
3. Hours of strenuous activity (lifting, carrying, shoveling) do not pose a problem for me.
4. I have been told that I have leadership qualities.
5. The idea of continuing study throughout my career appeals to me.
6. I am a logical and analytical thinker.
7. I enjoy working independently.

8. I function well as part of a team.
9. I believe professional ethics should be strictly adhered to.
10. I can live under primitive conditions in remote areas.

To consider yourself a potential archaeologist, you must see each statement as true. Even with just one false statement, you might want to reconsider your choice of field. Archaeology is an extremely rigorous and competitive profession.

Training

You must have a master's degree to qualify as a professional archaeologist, and a doctoral degree is often preferable. Most graduate programs in archaeology are found in anthropology departments, and some universities maintain schools of archaeology. Visit www.petersons.com for a list of available programs. To gain the necessary background on the undergraduate level, you should study anthropology, history, art, geology, or a related field. Your graduate studies should also include cultural and physical anthropology and linguistics.

Job Outlook and Salaries

There are relatively few openings in the field of teaching archaeology. However, federal grants and contracts provide more opportunities in archaeological fieldwork and research. A lot of this work is being conducted in the western and southwestern states, such as Colorado, Arizona, and New Mexico. Particularly in northwestern New Mexico, there is a strong industry developing resources such as gas and oil. Because much of the land there is owned by the Bureau of Land Management, the developers must hire professional archaeologists to clear the sites before gas lines or oil wells can be put in. Also, as construction projects increase, archaeologists will be needed to perform preliminary excavations in order to preserve historic sites.

In addition, the building of a reservoir on the Dolores River in Colorado uncovered hundreds of archaeological sites, necessitating a great deal of archaeological work. The project, which is the largest on the continent, has since brought many archaeologists to that area.

If you are a scholar who doesn't want a full-time professional career as an archaeologist but would like to experience archaeological work, you can find many opportunities to try working at a dig. If you are willing to invest your time and, in some cases, your money, you can find professionally supervised archaeological investigations that welcome volunteers. These are listed in *Archaeology* magazine or in the books mentioned at the end of this chapter.

In 2004, archaeologists had median annual earnings of $43,890.

Profiles

The profiles in this chapter include two archaeological sites and an archaeologist.

Fraser River Valley Archaeological Project

The Fraser River Valley Archaeological Project in British Columbia was initiated in June 2002. The focus of the project is the investigation of household and community organization, primarily Stó:lô plank and pithouse villages, in the Fraser River drainage east of Vancouver, BC.

The Stó:lô are a group of First Nations peoples who have inhabited the Fraser Valley for centuries. The name comes from the Halkomelem word for *river*, so the Stó:lô are called "the river people." Halkomelem is one of a family of languages spoken by the Coast Salish peoples.

The project is a joint endeavor by anthropologists and archaeologists from the University of California–Los Angeles, the University of British Columbia, Simon Fraser University, and the Stó:lô Nation. Rounding out the team are UCLA graduate students and student volunteers from UBC.

The archaeological team conducted exploratory work to relocate and investigate six late prehistoric and early historic village sites in the Fraser Valley, focusing on well-preserved early historic and later prehistoric pithouses in order to assess the condition of potential living floors and judge the caliber of preservation of artifacts. Artifacts of both aboriginal and Euro-Canadian origin were found, including nephrite adzes, slate knives, projectile points, abrading tools, a glass bead, and many metal and glass objects. The team also found preserved salmon and mammal bones. Additional features such as hearths and floor and subfloor deposits with wooden stake molds were found as well. These results, combined with the fact that the Stó:lô people have inhabited this land since the 1600s, suggest that the team may be able to gather solid data on household dynamics and variability, including analysis of architectural types, internal household organization and size, nature of participation in regional trade systems, and evidence for occupational specializations.

Crow Canyon Archaeological Center

Crow Canyon is a nonprofit research and educational institution funded by tuition, fees, donations, and federal grants. It comprises an eighty-acre campus in southwestern Colorado, near Mesa Verde National Park, with a staff of fifty or so archaeologists, educators, and support staff. In addition to their own research, staff archaeologists instruct adult and children participants who want to learn about archaeology. From junior high age on, participants are taken into the field and taught excavation, recording, and documentation techniques. They also work in the lab a few days a week learning analysis techniques and methods for cleaning artifacts.

Children too young for fieldwork can still participate in a simulated dig in a lab established for that purpose. There they can learn the same excavating techniques as they sift through large, shallow sand boxes where artifacts and walls and other features are buried, just as they would be in the field.

Participants come from all over North America on educational vacations and stay for a three- to five-day program. Crow Canyon also works with about a dozen graduate students of archaeology each year, providing rewarding internships. During the summer months, participants sleep in cabin tents or hogans, which are circular Navajo-style structures.

Montezuma County, where Crow Canyon is located, is home to more than ten thousand archaeological sites. Crow Canyon professionals have worked at more than twenty sites, concentrating their research on areas that were once Anasazi Indian villages. The Anasazi are the ancestors of present-day Pueblo Indians, who lived in this area of Colorado from the sixth century until about the year 1300, when they relocated to the south. The Crow Canyon team's research is focused on learning exactly when and why the Anasazi left the region; they are also investigating the political and social systems of the Anasazi.

For example, in March 2007, Crow Canyon began its third and final field season at Goodman Point Pueblo, a large village that served as the focal point of an extensive community during the mid- to late 1200s. The pueblo is one of forty-two sites located in the Goodman Point Unit of Hovenweep National Monument. Crow Canyon's excavations are conducted in partnership with the National Park Service, which manages the monument, and with the assistance of students and adults enrolled in research programs.

The fieldwork at Goodman Point Pueblo is the first phase of a larger research project called "The Goodman Point Archaeological

Project: Community Center and Cultural Landscape Study." The second phase of the study is scheduled for the 2008–2010 seasons and will include excavations at several surrounding sites within the unit, including habitation sites, ancient roadways, and agricultural fields.

Kristin Kuckelman—Senior Archaeologist

Kristin Kuckelman is a senior field archaeologist at Crow Canyon Archaeological Center. She has a bachelor's degree in anthropology and psychology from Colorado Women's College (which has now merged with the University of Denver) and earned her master's degree in anthropology with a concentration in archaeology from the University of Texas at Austin.

Getting Started. Kristin's interest in anthropology began when she was a child, traveling around the world with her military family. Her parents were interested in different cultures and in archaeology and passed that interest on to their daughter. When it came time for college, she was drawn to the anthropology program.

"I love the variety of it. I enjoy working outdoors. I enjoy writing," Kristin explains about her job. "And with any kind of research, there's the excitement of discovery. You're trying to solve problems. You're trying to find things out. You're trying to learn something new. And, basically, every time you go in the field, you hope you're going to learn something about a culture that no one knew before. You don't know what that's going to be; you never really know how it's going to turn out or what you're going to find."

She says that the sites in the area are very easy to discern. They have hundreds of masonry rooms, and even after centuries, there are telltale piles of rubble and thousands of artifacts scattered about the ground. Walking around the modern ground surface, you can see the tops of the walls and the depressions in the ground indicating the subterranean chambers.

Because of these subterranean chambers, the archaeologists sometimes have to dig down two and a half to three meters to find the actual floor of the structure. The surface rooms are shallower, but they can still require a meter or a meter and a half of digging.

The crews have found lithic artifacts, which are artifacts made out of stone, such as spear and arrow points, as well as sandstone tools for grinding grain. They have also unearthed tens of thousands of pottery fragments; intact pieces are very rarely found. Kristin explains that the crews very rarely engage in refitting, or trying to piece the shards together. With so many pieces scattered over the ground, it would take many years and would be very expensive and tedious work.

During the first week of May, which is the start of the field season, Kristin and her partner head out to the site, set up equipment, and make sure that the areas they want excavated are laid out and prepared. They take care of all the paperwork and mapping before the participants arrive to begin digging. Participants spend their first full day on campus, where they receive a full orientation about archaeology in general. They then spend two or three days a week in the field, where Kristin and her partner give them a site tour to provide a background on what it is they will be digging, why they are digging, and what they're trying to learn. They then receive tools and individual instruction and are placed, either individually or in pairs, at the particular places to be excavated.

Kristin explains that the basic procedure is to move dirt, put it in a bucket, and take it to a screening station. The dirt is sifted through a quarter-inch mesh screen to be sure the crew hasn't missed any artifacts. Everybody has his or her own bag to keep artifacts from each excavation area separate.

Near the end of the season, there is quite a bit of documentation and mapping to be done, and the artifacts must be washed and analyzed. Once the crews are finished with them, most of the artifacts are put in storage, though a few are rotated as exhibits at the Anasazi Heritage Center, a federally run curation facility. After this, the crews must fill the areas they've dug with all the screened dirt and rocks they originally dug out. For safety reasons, gaping holes can't be left in the land, and, in terms of conservation, leaving a pit open to the elements would damage the site. Before it is closed, the pit is lined with landscaping fabric to protect it and to provide a clue in case future archaeologists are digging there but do not have access to the earlier team's notes and maps. The lining would show them the site had already been excavated.

There are so many sites, and keeping a site open and developed for public exhibit, as has been done at Mesa Verde, would be extremely expensive. It would also be very hard on the architecture itself. Constant maintenance would have to be performed, or everything would eventually deteriorate.

During the winter, the archaeologists write reports on everything they learned the previous summer. They also write articles for professional journals and present papers at archaeological conferences across the country.

For Further Reading

The following are some suggestions for additional resources in archaeology.

Books and Guides

Archaeological Fieldwork Opportunities Bulletin (AFOB 2007). Boston: Archaeological Institute of America, Annual.

Fagan, Brian M. *Archaeology: A Brief Introduction*, 9th ed. Upper Saddle River, NJ: Prentice Hall, 2005.

Lewis, Barry, Lynn Kilgore, and Robert Jurmain. *Understanding Physical Anthropology and Archaeology*, 9th ed. Belmont, CA: Wadsworth Publishing, 2006.

Renfrew, Colin, and Paul Bahn. *Archaeology: Theories, Methods, and Practice*, 4th ed. London: Thames and Hudson, 2004.

Thomas, David Hurst, and Robert L. Kelly. *Archaeology*, 4th ed. Boston: Wadsworth Publishing, 2005.

Magazines
Archaeology, bimonthly
National Geographic, monthly
Scientific American, monthly
Smithsonian, monthly

Professional Journals
These journals, though not available in every local library, can be found in university libraries or in large public libraries. Some are available online; visit the websites for more information.

American Antiquity
Society for American Archaeology
www.saa.org

American Journal of Archaeology
Archaeological Institute of America
www.ajaonline.org

Historical Archaeology
Society for Historical Archaeology
www.sha.org

Journal of Anthropological Archaeology
Elsevier
www.elsevier.com/locate/jaa

Journal of Field Archaeology
Boston University
www.bu.edu/jfa

North American Archaeologist
Baywood Publishing Company
www.baywood.com

A Final Thought

Archaeology is a fascinating area for scholars who love to uncover the past as a way to learn more about the world and its peoples. If you'd like to combine your intellectual research skills with the opportunity to do some actual digging, you can build a successful and rewarding career in this challenging field.

CHAPTER SIX

Psychologists

Wh11hile some psychologists are clinicians, working in a therapeutic relationship with patients or clients, others study
human behavior and mental processes to understand,
explain, and change people's behavior. They may study the way a
person thinks, feels, or behaves. Research psychologists investigate
the physical, cognitive, emotional, or social aspects of human
behavior.

Like other social scientists, psychologists formulate hypotheses
and collect data to test their validity—their research methods
depend on the topic under study. Psychologists may gather information through controlled laboratory experiments; personality,
performance, aptitude, and intelligence tests; observation, interviews, and questionnaires; clinical studies; or surveys. Computers
are widely used to record and analyze this information.

Psychologists in applied fields counsel patients and conduct
training programs; conduct market research; apply psychological
treatments to a variety of medical and surgical conditions; or
provide mental health services in hospitals, clinics, and private
settings.

Psychology Disciplines

Because psychology deals with human behavior, psychologists
apply their knowledge and techniques to a wide range of endeavors, including human services, management, education, law, and

sports. In addition to the variety of work settings, psychologists specialize in many different areas.

- **Clinical psychologists,** who constitute the largest specialty, generally work in independent or group practice or in hospitals or clinics. They may help the mentally or emotionally disturbed adjust to life and are increasingly helping all kinds of medical and surgical patients deal with their illnesses or injuries. Some work in physical medicine and rehabilitation settings, treating patients with spinal cord injuries, chronic pain or illness, stroke, and arthritis and neurologic conditions, such as multiple sclerosis. Others help people deal with life stresses such as divorce or aging. Clinical psychologists interview patients; give diagnostic tests; provide individual, family, and group psychotherapy; and design and implement behavior modification programs. They may collaborate with physicians and other specialists in developing treatment programs and help patients understand and comply with the prescribed treatment. Some clinical psychologists work in universities, where they train graduate students in the delivery of mental health and behavioral medicine services. Others administer community mental health programs.
- **Counseling psychologists** perform many of the same functions as clinical psychologists and use several techniques, including interviewing and testing, to advise people on how to deal with problems of everyday living, whether personal, social, educational, or vocational.
- **Developmental psychologists** study the patterns and causes of behavioral change as people progress through life from infancy to adulthood. Some concern themselves with behavior during infancy, childhood, and adolescence, while others study changes that take place during maturity and old age. The study of developmental disabilities and how they affect

individuals and others is a new discipline within developmental psychology.

- **Educational psychologists** evaluate student and teacher needs and design and develop programs to enhance the educational setting.

- **School psychologists** work with students, teachers, parents, and administrators to resolve students' learning and behavior problems.

- **Experimental psychologists** study behavior processes and work with human beings and animals, such as rats, monkeys, and pigeons. Prominent areas of experimental research include motivation, thinking, attention, learning and retention, sensory and perceptual processes, effects of substance use and abuse, and genetic and neurological factors in behavior.

- **Industrial and organizational psychologists** apply psychological techniques to personnel administration, management, and marketing problems. They are involved in policy planning, applicant screening, training and development, psychological testing research, counseling, and organizational development and analysis. For example, an industrial psychologist may work with management to develop better training programs and to reorganize the work setting to improve worker productivity or quality of work life.

- **Social psychologists** examine people's interactions with others and with the social environment. Prominent areas of study include group behavior, leadership, attitudes, and interpersonal perception.

The past few years have seen a rise in some newer specialties:

- **Cognitive psychologists** deal with the brain's role in memory, thinking, and perceptions; some are involved with research related to computer programming and artificial intelligence.

- **Health psychologists** promote good health through health maintenance counseling programs that are designed, for example, to help people stop smoking or lose weight.
- **Neuropsychologists** study the relation between the brain and behavior. They often work in stroke and head-injury programs.
- **Geropsychologists** deal with the special problems faced by the elderly.

The emergence and growth of these specialties reflects the increasing participation of psychologists in providing direct services to special patient populations.

Other areas of specialization include psychometrics, history of psychology, art therapy, psychopharmacology, and community, comparative, consumer, engineering, environmental, family, forensic, population, military, and rehabilitation psychology. Many psychologists also hold faculty positions at colleges and universities and some work as high school psychology teachers.

Working Conditions

A psychologist's specialty and place of employment determine working conditions. For example, clinical, school, and counseling psychologists in private practice have pleasant, comfortable offices and can set their own hours, but they often work evening hours to accommodate their clients. Some employed in hospitals, nursing homes, and other health facilities work evenings and weekends, while others in schools and clinics work regular hours. Psychologists employed by academic institutions divide their hours among teaching, research, and administrative responsibilities. Some also maintain part-time consulting practices. In contrast to the many psychologists who have flexible work schedules, most who practice in government and private industry have more structured schedules.

Reading and writing research reports is often solitary work, and psychologists may experience the pressures of deadlines, tight schedules, and overtime work. Their routines may be interrupted frequently, and travel may be required to attend conferences or conduct research.

After several years of experience, some psychologists, usually those with doctoral degrees, enter private practice or set up their own research or consulting firms. A growing proportion of psychologists are self-employed.

Job Outlook

Psychologists held about 179,000 jobs in 2004. Educational institutions employed about one out of four psychologists in positions other than teaching, such as counseling, testing, research, and administration. About two out of ten were employed in health care, primarily in offices of mental health practitioners, physicians' offices, outpatient mental health clinics, substance abuse centers, and private hospitals. Government agencies at the state and local levels employed psychologists in public hospitals, clinics, correctional facilities, and other settings.

The outlook for this field is very good. Employment of psychologists is expected to increase between 18 and 26 percent through 2014, based on increased demand for psychological services in schools, hospitals, social service agencies, mental health centers, substance abuse treatment clinics, consulting firms, and private companies.

Among the specialties, job opportunities should be best for school psychologists, especially those with a specialist degree or higher. Growing awareness of how students' mental health and behavioral problems, such as bullying, affect learning is increasing demand for school psychologists to offer student counseling and mental health services.

Clinical and counseling psychologists will be needed to help people deal with depression and other mental disorders, marriage and family problems, job stress, and addiction. The rise in health care costs associated with unhealthy lifestyles, such as smoking, alcoholism, and obesity, has made prevention and treatment more critical. An increase in the number of employee assistance programs, which help workers deal with personal problems, also should spur job growth in these specialties.

Industrial and organizational psychologists will be in demand to help boost worker productivity and retention rates in a wide range of businesses. They will help companies deal with issues such as workplace diversity and antidiscrimination policies. Companies also will use psychologists' expertise in survey design, analysis, and research to develop tools for marketing evaluation and statistical analysis.

Demand should be particularly strong for professionals who hold doctorates from leading universities in applied specialties, such as counseling, health, and school psychology. Those with extensive training in quantitative research methods and computer science may have a competitive edge over applicants without such experience.

Psychologists with master's degrees in fields other than industrial or organizational psychology will face keen competition for jobs because of the limited number of positions that require only a master's degree. They may find jobs as psychological assistants or counselors, providing mental health services under the direct supervision of a licensed psychologist. Still others may find jobs involving research and data collection and analysis in universities, government, or private companies.

Opportunities directly related to psychology will be limited for bachelor's degree holders. Some may find jobs as assistants in rehabilitation centers or in other jobs involving data collection and analysis. Those who meet state certification requirements may become high school psychology teachers.

. . . .

Training

You generally need a doctoral degree to work as an independent licensed clinical or counseling psychologist. A Ph.D. qualifies you for a wide range of teaching, research, clinical, and counseling positions in universities, health care services, elementary and secondary schools, private industry, and government. A doctor of psychology (Psy.D.) degree is valuable if you plan to work in clinical positions or in private practice, but you might also sometime teach, conduct research, or carry out administrative responsibilities.

A doctoral degree requires five to seven years of graduate study, culminating in a dissertation based on original research. Courses in quantitative research methods, including the use of computer-based analysis, will be an integral part of your graduate program and are necessary to complete your dissertation. A Psy.D. may be based on practical work and examinations rather than a dissertation. In clinical or counseling psychology, your requirements for the doctoral degree will include at least a one-year internship.

If you plan to work as a school psychologist, you will most likely need a specialist degree, although a few states still credential school psychologists with master's degrees. A specialist (Ed.S.) degree in school psychology requires a minimum of three years of full-time graduate study (at least sixty graduate semester hours) and a one-year internship. Because your professional practice will address educational and mental health components of students' development, your training as a school psychologist will include course work in both education and psychology.

Once you earn a master's degree, you may work as an industrial or organizational psychologist. You could also qualify to work as a psychological assistant under the supervision of doctoral-level psychologists and may conduct research or psychological evaluations. A master's degree in psychology requires at least two years of full-time graduate study, which includes practical experience in an applied setting and a master's thesis based on an original research project.

Competition for admission to graduate psychology programs is keen. Some universities require that you have an undergraduate major in psychology. Others prefer only course work in basic psychology with courses in the biological, physical, and social sciences and in statistics and mathematics.

With a bachelor's degree in psychology, you are qualified to assist psychologists and other professionals in community mental health centers, vocational rehabilitation offices, and correctional programs. You may also work as a research or administrative assistant for psychologists. In addition, you may find work in related fields, such as marketing research, or in another area, such as sales or business management.

You are qualified to work in entry-level positions for the federal government with at least twenty-four semester hours in psychology and one course in statistics. However, you'll most likely face stiff competition for these jobs because this is one of the few areas in which one can work as a psychologist without an advanced degree.

The American Psychological Association (APA) presently accredits doctoral training programs in clinical, counseling, and school psychology, as well as institutions that provide internships for doctoral students in school, clinical, and counseling psychology. The National Association of School Psychologists, with the assistance of the National Council for Accreditation of Teacher Education, also is involved in the accreditation of advanced degree programs in school psychology. The Canadian Psychological Association (CPA) accredits doctoral programs and internships in professional areas of psychology.

Psychologists in independent practice or those who offer any type of patient care—including clinical, counseling, and school psychologists—must meet certification or licensing requirements in all states, provinces, and the District of Columbia. Licensing laws vary by locality and by type of position and require licensed or certified psychologists to limit their practice to areas in which they have developed professional competence through training and experience. Practice in clinical and counseling psychology usually requires a doctorate in psychology, the completion of an approved internship, and one to two years of professional experience. In addition, all jurisdictions require that applicants pass an examination. Most licensing boards administer a standardized test, and many supplement that with additional oral or essay questions. Some require continuing education for renewal of the license. Both the American Psychological Association and the Canadian Psychological Association offer continuing education opportunities, such as seminars and workshops, online courses, and mentoring programs.

The National Association of School Psychologists (NASP) awards the Nationally Certified School Psychologist (NCSP) designation, which recognizes professional competency in school psychology at a national, rather than state, level. Currently, twenty-six states recognize the NCSP and allow those with the certification to transfer credentials from one state to another without taking a new exam. In those states, the requirements for certification or licensure and those for the NCSP often are the same or similar. Requirements for the NCSP certification include the completion of sixty graduate semester hours in school psychology; a twelve-hundred-hour internship, six hundred hours of which must be completed in a school setting; and a passing score on the National School Psychology Examination.

The American Board of Professional Psychology (ABPP) recognizes professional achievement by awarding certification in clinical psychology, clinical neuropsychology, and counseling, forensic, industrial, organizational, and school psychology. Candidates for ABPP certification need a doctorate, postdoctoral training in their specialty, five years of experience, professional endorsements, and a passing grade on an examination.

Aspiring psychologists who are interested in direct patient care must be emotionally stable, mature, and able to deal effectively with people. Sensitivity, compassion, good communication skills, and the ability to lead and inspire others are particularly important qualities for those wishing to do clinical work and counseling. Research psychologists should be able to do detailed work both independently and as part of a team. Patience and perseverance are vital qualities because achieving results in the psychological treatment of patients or in research may take a long time.

Salaries

Median annual earnings of wage and salary clinical, counseling, and school psychologists were $54,950 in 2004. The majority earned between $41,850 and $71,880. The lowest 10 percent earned less than $32,280, and the highest 10 percent earned more than $92,250.

Median annual earnings in the industries employing the largest numbers of clinical, counseling, and school psychologists were as follows:

Offices of other health practitioners	$64,460
Elementary and secondary schools	$58,360
Outpatient care centers	$46,850
Individual and family services	$42,640

Median annual earnings of wage and salary industrial and organizational psychologists in 2004 were $71,400. The middle 50 percent earned between $56,880 and $93,210. The lowest 10 percent earned less than $45,620, and the highest 10 percent earned more than $125,560.

......

Profiles

Read the following real-life accounts from two psychologists to see whether this might be the right field for you.

Denise Stybr—School Psychologist

Denise Stybr has been a school psychologist with the Center Cass School District in Downers Grove, Illinois, since 1990. She earned a B.S. in psychology from the University of Illinois, Urbana, and an M.S. in school psychology from Governors State University in University Park, Illinois. She began her professional career in 1982.

Her duties include administering psychoeducational testing to determine the presence or absence of a disabling condition, such as a learning disability, mental retardation, or emotional disorder. She also provides individual and group counseling to the students, consults with the parents and staff, and designs behavior management programs.

Denise describes her job as extremely stressful but never boring, since she makes life-changing decisions that affect both children and their families. She works from 7:30 A.M. until 4:30 P.M., and the days are always full. She is often met in the parking lot with questions and concerns, and she regularly works a whole day with only a half-hour break for lunch. On a typical day she attends several meetings that focus on deciding whether a child should be tested and whether he or she qualifies for services after the tests have been completed. She also presents test results to the child's parents.

Between meetings, she usually holds two to three counseling sessions, spends two to three hours testing, and spends the remainder of the time writing reports and talking to teachers or parents. She travels to three schools, often on the same day.

Denise admits that she doesn't like the stress level or the too-frequent feeling that whatever she does isn't going to be enough for a child. But she does like the freedom and variety of the job—she rarely has to do any one thing at a specific time (with the exception of meetings), and she can choose when to do her other tasks.

Getting Started. Denise originally planned to become a psychiatrist, but by junior year of college decided that medical school was not for her. She researched the different areas of graduate study for psychology and liked the freedom that school psychology offered. She doesn't have to maintain her own office or records or purchase malpractice insurance. She doesn't have to get coverage to take a vacation, and she never has to turn away someone who needs help but can't pay. Most of her work is with children ages three to fourteen, an age range in which it's relatively easy to make progress.

Denise explains that in order to practice as a certified school psychologist you must also complete a school-year internship, during which you act as a school psychologist but are closely supervised by a certified school psychologist. In addition, you must complete seventy-five contact hours of continuing educational activities every three years in order to maintain your national certification.

The reason Denise has a B.S. instead of a B.A. is that she originally planned to attend medical school, so she took more science courses than required for a B.A. Her M.S. is a specialist degree, which required fifty-seven or more hours, unlike a regular master's that requires thirty to thirty-two hours.

Advice from a Professional. Denise has found that working as a school psychologist requires a certain personality type almost more than it does any special talent. You must be structured and organized but still remain flexible, and you must know when to take a stand and when to back down. You must have empathy, but not sympathy, and compassion without sentimentality. A school psychologist often works with no peer input and must remain impartial.

She recommends looking for after-school and summer jobs that put you around children and their parents. If possible, volunteer with developmentally disabled children in order to see if you have what it takes to work with that population. You can also ask to observe in some special education classrooms.

She also advises being realistic about your financial expectations. School psychologists often are paid lower salaries than teachers and may not receive the same benefits. They generally work longer days than teachers, and they often work during the summer and for a week or two before school starts and after school ends.

"This is not an easy, high-paying job," she says. "It is truly a vocation more than an occupation."

Gerald D. Oster—Clinical Psychologist

Gerald D. Oster is a licensed psychologist with a private practice. He is also a clinical associate professor of psychiatry at the University of Maryland Medical School in Baltimore.

He earned his B.A. in sociology at the University of South Florida, Tampa; his M.A. in psychology at Middle Tennessee State University in Murfreesboro; and his Ph.D. in psychology at Virginia Commonwealth University in Richmond.

The Work. Dr. Oster points out that he consciously set out to have several jobs because he enjoys variety, and his career allows him to experience a great deal of variety in his workdays. For instance, on Monday he works at home and in his private practice. On Tuesday morning he spends two hours at a community mental health center in the inner city of Baltimore, where he works as a child and family therapist. His two current patients are an adolescent and a young child. One is a sixteen-year-old boy who has served time in juvenile delinquent centers and now is trying to reenter the community but is struggling to fit in at school and in his foster-care placement. The other is a boy in kindergarten who is very insecure about his environment. He lives in a dangerous neighborhood with his grandparents as his primary caretakers. His mother, who also lives with him, is a drug addict. When he is not working with these two patients, he is doing the large amount of paperwork required by the various governing agencies that monitor the clinic.

After catching up at the clinic, he spends eight hours at the University Counseling Center, where he sees the opposite end of the spectrum—very intelligent and creative people who are in various professional schools, such as law, medicine, or social work. Although quite articulate and resourceful, they have their own struggles and often make good use of the support that the center provides. Most visit the center primarily because of the stress of school but also due to problems in relationships or in the caretaking of others (many are married or have relatives or children that they are responsible for). Also, the pace and expectations for learning are incredible and require a huge sacrifice socially that many have a difficult time adjusting to. After these hours are over, Dr. Oster usually goes to his private practice to sort through the mail or see an occasional evening patient.

His other days are similar, but each involves different demands and different populations. He may spend time at the local community hospital, interviewing or testing a suicidal or out-of-control adolescent. His private practice is devoted to seeing children and adults with an assortment of problems that might stem from family discord, learning difficulties in school and their emotional impact, or relationship problems.

Although he is always busy, Dr. Oster says that he still has to look for new ways to maintain his practice, especially in the context of managed care. For many clinical psychologists in private practice, the paperwork and payment problems of managed care have become quite difficult. This has also affected the hospitals where he works and has created uncertainty in many of the health professions.

Getting Started. Gerald Oster began his undergraduate studies as a business major, but he found that courses in sociology were much more appealing, and his thinking and viewpoints were similar to those of the sociology students and faculty. He was intrigued by the prospect of studying topics such as social and political theory and how people adapt to environmental and economic change. The prospect of studying these topics on a higher level was challenging as well.

He says, "Learning about and helping people in all aspects of life filled a need in myself to go beyond my own boundaries and provide support to people in stress or to help the broader institutions in gaining the appropriate placement for people who needed assistance, whether it was the aged, juvenile delinquents, or children with learning problems."

The decision to pursue a career in clinical psychology didn't occur until after he received his undergraduate degree and owned a bookstore for several years. He believes that this waiting period is not unique, and that only a few students have a specific direction regarding careers. Rather than graduating from college with the hope of just getting a job, career choice means much more. He feels that it is something that you know you love and want to pursue full-time; in essence, it becomes a paid hobby.

Once he realized that psychology was his career choice, he still had to decide which specialty to pursue. He initially chose criminal psychology and was fascinated by courses in personality, psychopathology, and child development. This led to his master's degree and to work in the juvenile justice system, providing evaluations for the courts on delinquents. However, through the support of his professors and continuing interest in all of psychology, he applied and was accepted into a doctoral program where he was exposed to a greater depth and breadth of psychology.

During his doctoral studies, he worked in a rat laboratory, was part of a developing center for aging, taught courses in developmental psychology and child development, and was exposed to continuing clinical work through practicums at child development centers and psychiatric units for the aged. He also participated with many research teams on topics of learning theory, intellectual testing, and cognitive changes over the life span.

His professional career began in 1981 at a private research firm that subcontracted work from the National Institutes of Health (NIH), where he was involved in coordinating research projects for a nationwide study on depression. After a year, he decided to return to clinical work and obtained a job as a psychologist in the adolescent unit of a state hospital. During that time, he also consulted to a geriatric unit and continued his own learning through weekly seminars and clinical rounds.

After several years of practice and earning his independent professional license, he changed locations and began working at a residential treatment center for emotionally disturbed children and adolescents, where he became director of psychology internship training. He also continued his own training, which included study in family therapy at a well-known institute. He then became interested in expanding his private practice and continuing the writing he had begun during this time, so he resigned and began collecting a series of part-time jobs.

Dr. Oster has authored or coauthored a number of professional books on psychological testing and therapy. He also cowrote a trade book, *Helping Your Depressed Teenager: A Guide for Parents and Caregivers* (Wiley, 1995). His most recent book is *Life as a Psychologist: Career Choices and Insights* (Routledge, 2004).

Advice from a Professional. "Learning is a lifelong process. Degrees only give you permission to learn," says Dr. Oster. He advises that you should expect to change career paths several times, and that going to college and possibly to graduate school allows you to gather technical skills as well as to explore possibilities. A field such as psychology offers numerous outlets to pursue, and along the way, you can define yourself in many ways.

Dr. Oster recommends sticking to a broad path and realizing that the path may have many branches. While they are all quite good, it takes exposure to these branches to realize the possibilities. Read articles from journals or magazines by people who are doing the kind of work you can see yourself doing, and learn what is exciting and meaningful to you. Don't be afraid to contact these people or talk with your professors, who want to help and have placed themselves as models and as valuable resources.

He also suggests gaining experience wherever you can through paid or volunteer work. Attend seminars and conventions, even if they are supposed to be for professionals, because they are the best way to learn about the possibilities within a profession. You'll gain incredible exposure and an awareness of what the field is all about.

It's also a good idea to gain mentors along the way. Becoming an assistant, whether in teaching or research, is an excellent way to discover your strengths and weaknesses and to learn whether you could see yourself doing this work on a daily basis. You should also pursue as many practicums or internships as possible.

Dr. Oster also recommends traveling. He says, "In striving for an ideal picture of yourself, you also want to be aware of possible settings. Do you enjoy the outdoors or city life? Does your profession offer more possibilities in small towns, where you actually perform more duties, than in large cities, where there are many specialists but more people, job opportunities, and so on. What type of atmosphere do you prefer—the pressure of the Northeast or the slower pace of the South or the alternative lifestyles of the Southwest?"

For Further Reading

There are many books you can consult for additional information in the areas of psychology. Following are a few examples to get you started.

Landy, Frank L., and Jeffrey M. Conte. *Work in the 21st Century: An Introduction to Industrial and Organizational Psychology,* 2nd ed. New York: Wiley, 2006.

Morgan, Robert D. *Life After Psychology Graduate School: Insider's Advice from New Psychologists.* New York: Psychology Press, 2004.

Prout, H. Thompson, and Douglas T. Brown, Eds. *Counseling and Psychotherapy with Children and Adolescents: Theory and Practice for School and Clinical Settings,* 4th ed. New York: Wiley, 2007.

Slater, Alan, and Gavin Bremner. *An Introduction to Developmental Psychology.* New York: Wiley, 2003.

Sternberg, Robert J. *Career Paths in Psychology: Where Your Degree Can Take You,* 2nd ed. Washington, DC: American Psychological Association, 2006.

A Final Thought

Although psychology may sound like a single career option, you now know that the field of psychology encompasses a number of specializations. Any one of these would be an appropriate and rewarding career choice for a scholar who wants to help others who are in need.

CHAPTER SEVEN

Museum Curators

I f you ask some people what they think of museums, they might tell you that the word conjures up images of yawn-stifling tours in quiet, tomblike places, the atmosphere as inspiring as the inside of a crypt. The idea of displaying and examining the art and artifacts that make up the world's history reminds them of dry school lessons filled with impossible-to-remember names and dates and events that hold no meaning in their current lives.

Fortunately, that perception is not as widely shared as those uninitiated in the wonder of museums might believe. But if you are reading this book, you already know that. Museums are not dull and lifeless structures displaying dull and lifeless artifacts. They are as exciting as a space launch or a Civil War battlefield, an African safari or a Roman amphitheater.

Patrons of the arts, history lovers, and those who look to the future have continuously provided enthusiastic support to museums, ensuring their survival through the ages. From meager beginnings, thousands of museums now flourish throughout the world, displaying a wide range of collections.

Museums are no longer repositories for just art or ancient relics. They house everything from moon rocks to Julia Childs's kitchen. And as varied as the collections are, so are the opportunities for employment. In this chapter we explore the different kinds of museums and the career paths they offer.

The Different Kinds of Museums

Today, there are as many different kinds of museums as the topics they explain or the items they display. Some are famous, such as the museums of the Smithsonian Institution; others are small establishments, known only locally. This chapter gives you an overview of each type of museum.

Art Museums

Art museums are buildings where objects of aesthetic value are preserved and displayed. Art museums have a variety of functions, including acquiring, conserving, and exhibiting works of art; providing art education for the general public; and conducting art historical research.

Since the beginning of the twentieth century, art museums have seen a number of trends, such as the expansion of large institutions and the creation of a horde of specialized museums, many of which are devoted to modern art. In contrast, a number of the world's largest museums have begun to reduce their size and improve the quality of their collections. They accomplish this by selling less-important works of art in order to concentrate available funds on acquiring works of greater artistic merit or historical significance.

Art Galleries

Art galleries are generally privately owned, and some are similar to specialized museums in which the collection is restricted to the works of a single artist. Art galleries can also focus on a specific historical period, category of art, or geographical region.

History Museums

From acquiring collections and preserving them to explaining and displaying them, the dedicated professionals employed in history museums have the chance to work with every aspect of the relics and other forms of physical evidence of the past. History museums can cover a particular period, such as Colonial America, or a particular topic, such as entertainment or advertising.

A history museum's collection could be displayed in a modern building constructed specifically for that purpose, or the building itself, along with its contents, could be historical. Examples include the homes of famous people such as Paul Revere or Thomas Jefferson or historic structures such as lighthouses or old courthouses.

Living History Museums

A living history museum is a vibrant, active village, town, or city where the day-to-day life of a particular time period has been authentically re-created. The houses and public buildings are restored originals or thoroughly researched reproductions. Interiors are outfitted with period furniture, cookware, bed linens, and tablecloths.

Employees known as character interpreters function as residents, wearing the clothing of the day and discussing their dreams and concerns with visitors as they go about their daily tasks. If you were to stop a costumed gentleman passing by and ask where the nearest McDonald's is, he might direct you to a neighbor's farm. He might even do so using the dialect of his home country.

Colonial Williamsburg in Virginia and Plimoth Plantation in Massachusetts are just two examples of living history museums. These large enterprises offer employment for professional and entry-level workers in a wide variety of categories.

Natural History Museums

Natural history museums are dedicated to research, exhibition, and education in the natural sciences. Natural history museums vary in size and collections and could include all or some of the following departments: anthropology, astronomy, botany, entomology, fossil and living vertebrates, geology, herpetology and ichthyology, mammalogy, mineralogy, ornithology, and vertebrate paleontology.

Collections in natural history musuems may include artifacts from ancient civilizations, gems and jewels, fossils and skeletons, meteorites, and animals from around the world displayed in life-like settings.

Science Museums and Discovery Centers

Science museums preserve and display objects that have been important to the development of science and technology. Science centers, or discovery centers, as they are sometimes called, generally teach the principles related to these fields and often involve visitors in hands-on activities, many catering particularly to children. The two types of science institutions are not mutually exclusive, although most fall into one category or the other.

Planetariums

Planetariums are structures, usually with domed ceilings, that are outfitted to give audiences the illusion of being outside under a starlit sky. Through the use of projectors, slides, movies, and computers, the locations of the planets and stars and all other sorts of astronomical activity can be demonstrated.

Planetariums are often part of a science museum complex, with most large cities now having full-scale facilities. They are used as tourist and educational attractions with elaborate space exhibits or public observational facilities. Smaller planetariums are also associated with universities and are used for classroom instruction in geography, navigation, and astronomy.

National Monuments

National monuments, such as the Statue of Liberty and Ellis Island, are operated by the National Park Service, which falls under the umbrella of the U.S. Department of the Interior. These federally funded museums offer a wide range of full-time and seasonal employment for interpretive rangers and other personnel.

Canada's extensive national park system has nearly one thousand sites throughout the country. Sites such as the Carleton Martello Tower and Green Gables House are maintained and operated by Parks Canada.

Jobs in Museums

Professional job classifications in museums can fall into several categories, including administration, collections, curation, education and interpretation, development (fund-raising), exhibit design, and research.

Many job titles are common to each kind of museum, but the job description varies depending on the institution. Curators, exhibit designers, and researchers, for example, are found in almost every kind of museum, from art to science and history museums, even though the collections they deal with and their specific duties are very different.

Curators are specialists in a particular academic discipline relevant to a museum's collections. They are generally responsible for the care and interpretation of all objects and specimens on loan or belonging to the museum, and they are fully knowledgeable about each object's history and importance.

Depending upon the museum and their own areas of interest, curators can work with textiles and costumes, paintings, memorabilia, historic structures, crafts, furniture, coins, or a variety of other historically significant items.

Qualifications

To find work as a curator, you generally need a master's degree in an appropriate discipline within the museum's specialty—art history, history, archaeology—or in museum studies. You may even need a doctoral degree, particularly in natural history or science museums. Earning two graduate degrees—in museum studies (museology) and in a specialized subject—gives you a distinct advantage in this competitive job market.

You may be able to find a position with only a bachelor's degree in a small museum. For some positions, you need to complete an internship of full-time museum work supplemented by courses in museum practices.

Curatorial positions often require knowledge in a number of fields. For historic and artistic conservation, you should take courses in chemistry, physics, and art. Because curators, particularly those in small museums, may have administrative and managerial responsibilities, courses in business administration, public relations, marketing, and fund-raising also are recommended. Computer skills and the ability to work with electronic databases are essential. Many curators are responsible for posting information on the Internet, so you should be familiar with digital imaging, scanning technology, and copyright law.

Curators must be flexible because of their wide variety of duties, among which are the design and presentation of exhibits. In small museums, curators need manual dexterity to build exhibits or restore objects. Leadership ability and business skills are important for museum directors, while marketing skills are valuable in increasing museum attendance and fund-raising. Curators must have the ability to explain and interpret the collections to the public and be familiar with the techniques of selection, evaluation, preservation, restoration, and exhibition of the museum's collections.

In large museums, curators may advance through several levels of responsibility, eventually becoming the museum director. Curators in smaller museums often advance to larger ones. Individual research and publications are important for advancement in larger institutions. Three years of experience in a museum or related educational or research facility would usually be required before a candidate could advance to a full curatorial position.

. . . .

Training

How you proceed will depend on your interests and circumstances. If you are clear from the start about which avenue you wish to pursue, you can create your course of study at the university of your choosing by taking the appropriate courses. This type of educational background still serves as the main foundation for successful museum work. However, for the last thirty years or so, more and more people have completed university programs that offer practical and theoretical training in museum studies. Courses such as museum management, curatorship, fund-raising, exhibition development, and law and museums offer a more specific approach to the work at hand. Coupled with a broad background in liberal arts or specialization in an academic discipline, this training provides museum professionals with a base of knowledge designed to serve the needs of the museum.

Whatever your course of study, you'll find that most museums require an upper-level degree, either in an academic discipline or in museum studies, museum science, or museology. Also required is an intensive internship or record of long-term volunteer work.

What follows are three possible tracks with which you can proceed to prepare for a career in museums:

TRACK I
- Bachelor's degree in general museum studies, museology, or museum science
- Master's degree or doctorate in a specific academic discipline
- Internship arranged through the university or directly with a museum in a particular field

TRACK 2
- Bachelor's degree in liberal arts or a specific discipline
- Master's degree or certificate in museum studies, museology, or museum science
- Internship arranged through the university or directly with a museum in a particular field

TRACK 3 (for the museum professional changing careers or upgrading skills)
- Master's degree or certificate in museum studies or noncredit certificate in museum studies (short-term course)

The internship is considered the most crucial practical learning experience and is generally a requirement in all programs. It can run from ten weeks to a year with varying time commitments per week.

Salaries

A beginning curator who has almost completed a Ph.D. would start somewhere in mid-thirties. Smithsonian staff are employees of the federal government and follow the General Schedule (GS) pay scale. A supervisory museum curator, a job that requires specialized experience, could start at over $100,000.

In 2004, median annual earnings of curators were $43,620, with the majority earning between $32,790 and $58,280. The lowest 10 percent earned less than $25,360, and the highest 10 percent earned more than $77,490. In 2005, the average annual salary of curators in the federal government was $76,126.

Profiles

The following museum professionals have shared their experiences. Read about their careers to see what the work is really like.

Charles McGovern—Curator

Charles McGovern works at the National Museum of American History, part of the Smithsonian Institution complex in Washington, D.C., that is devoted to the exhibition, care, and study of artifacts that reflect the experience of the American people. He is supervisor of the American History Museum's Division of Community Life, overseeing a group of technicians, specialists, collections-based researchers, curators, and support staff. He is also a curator, responsible for Twentieth Century Consumerism and Popular Culture Department, which covers the history of entertainment, leisure, recreation, and commerce.

Charles graduated from Swarthmore College in Pennsylvania with a B.A. with honors in history and immediately entered graduate school at Harvard and earned his A.M. in history and his Ph.D. in American civilization.

Getting Started. Charles taught history at Harvard during his graduate studies and also was a research fellow at the Smithsonian. After completing his education, he returned to the Smithsonian as a full-time curator.

His interest in cultural history began at an early age. He watched a lot of television and listened to the radio and was part of the mass popular culture of the 1960s. His parents told him stories about the early days of radio. In high school, reading books his teachers recommended, he realized that Babe Ruth and Laurel and Hardy and the Marx brothers, personalities he cared very deeply about, were as much a part of history as Franklin Delano Roosevelt or World War I.

The Work. As a curator, Charles is a historian who must be able to understand and explain the lives and beliefs of our ancestors. He says that at the Smithsonian, "We try to do that respectfully, understanding the world as they saw it. As we do that, we see how culture reflects the times, the fears and ideals and problems of a given society. You cannot look at certain creations of our popular culture without seeing those kinds of elements in them."

He documents the history of the everyday life of American people and is responsible for the creation and maintenance of the collections in his area. His job is divided into three specific parts: acquisition of new objects and exhibits, exhibits and interpretion, and research. His primary job duties are to oversee the building collections, develop exhibitions, conduct research, write, speak publicly, and act as graduate advisor to eleven research fellows.

The collections that Charles is responsible for include a fascinating variety of objects. The exhibits that comprise Twentieth Century Consumerism and Popular Culture are probably the most popular and well-known in the museum. Visitors come to view Judy Garland's ruby slippers from *The Wizard of Oz*, Archie Bunker's well-worn chair, and the original Kermit the Frog puppet. There are a hat that Jimmy Durante used in his stage appearances; Howdy Doody; Mr. Moose and Bunny Rabbit and the Grandfather clock from the Captain Kangaroo show; the sweater worn by Mister Rogers; the leather jacket and hat worn by Harrison Ford in the Indiana Jones films; the Hawaiian shirt, baseball cap, and ring that Tom Selleck wore as Magnum, P. I.; old 78 rpm records; movie posters; and comic books.

As curator, Charles looks for items that provide insight into American consumerism and commerce. The collections include the bonnet worn by the woman who posed for the Sunmaid raisin box, a huge collection of turn-of-the-century advertising and marketing, and a collection of memorabilia from the world fairs of 1851 to 1988.

Most of the items in the collections have been donated to the museum. Charles explains that the museum has a very small budget for acquisitions and is therefore unable to compete with private galleries. As he says, "People must be willing to donate, so we look for people who either don't need the money or get the point of what we're trying to do."

Despite the best intentions, however, not every item that is offered can be accepted. Charles describes the case of Charlie Chaplin's cane: "Someone called once and wanted to donate Charlie Chaplin's cane. But first, how do I know that it was his cane? It's impossible to document that. And second, Chaplin probably went through thousands of canes. Those bamboo things snapped very easily. Something like that we couldn't take."

This story points to one very important aspect of Charles's job as curator—the ability to document items. He must be familiar with the history of every object in the collection, and the number of items is staggering. As he says, "It's not as if I were a curator of paintings where I'm trained in oils and brush techniques. Once in a while I have to confer with an appraiser or dealer to determine authenticity."

Given the size of the collection, it is not possible for all items to be exhibited simultaneously. Charles explains that less than 2 percent of the collection is on display at any time, and the rest is kept in storage. While some of the most famous items, such as Dorothy's ruby slippers or Archie Bunker's chair, on are permanent display, others rotate.

It is Charles's responsibility to decide which items are exhibited, stored, and rotated. He must also see that the items are cared for to avoid deterioration. This requires occasional removal of even the most popular items, a fact that doesn't always please the paying public. Charles explains that most visitors to the museum expect to see specific items and are disappointed if they are not on exhibit.

He says that the exhibiting part of the job is a team effort. As curator, he works with exhibit designers to decide how an item should be displayed. The designer plans the layout of the object and the accompanying text, graphics, and props. The care and maintenance of the item is the responsibility of a conservator, who also determines things such as the maximum amount of light to which an item can be exposed to avoid deterioration.

While the exhibits are the most public part of Charles's job, he feels that research is actually his primary duty. In his opinion, "All the collecting and exhibiting doesn't mean anything unless you have something to say. You have to figure out first what point you're making. Our point is the showing of everyday life of the American people, and for earlier times, that's something that has to be researched. Of course, you do research to support the things you already have in your collection, but the research also helps you to determine what you should be out there collecting."

The Smithsonian as Training Ground. Every year the Smithsonian awards dozens of research fellowships, providing funding and access to museum collections for Ph.D. candidates. To be hired as a curator, a candidate must possess or be near completion of a Ph.D. Entry-level positions include technicians and specialists and research-related jobs. Paid internships and volunteer positions are usually available and are a good way to get a foot in the door.

Charles McGovern points out that jobs for curators at the Smithsonian seldom become available. But because the Smithsonian has a certain reputation and skill in training, it is a good place to gain a foundation and then go out to other areas or institutions for work. An internship at the Smithsonian will go a long way in securing employment elsewhere. He believes that because of the Smithsonian's size, sometimes more really interesting work gets done in smaller museums with a more fixed mission.

Erica Hirshler—Curator of Paintings

Erica Hirshler is the Croll Senior Curator of Paintings, Art of the Americas, at the Museum of Fine Arts in Boston. She earned her B.A. from Wellesley College in art history and medieval studies, as well as her M.A. in art history, a museum studies diploma, and a Ph.D. in art history from Boston University.

Erica began at the Museum of Fine Arts as a volunteer, and only four months later she was offered a paying, part-time job. Two years later that developed into a full-time position as assistant curator, which is the job she describes here.

The Work. As assistant curator, Erica worked with a collection of two thousand paintings. The departmental structure includes the curator, an associate curator, an assistant curator, and four research assistants and fellows with various areas of specialization. Erica handled a wide range of duties, including working on the permanent collection; organizing special exhibits; conducting research; writing catalogs, art books, and copy for exhibition brochures; administering loan requests; and arranging for the display of various items in the galleries. She also responded to a large amount of correspondence, answering inquiries that ranged from a private citizen curious about the history of a family-owned painting to a scholar needing information for a project at another institution.

Erica describes what she liked most about the job. "I like working with the objects. It's a special thrill working with the real thing that you don't get from slides. I'm interested in them as physical objects. You gather them together for a special exhibition; you get to really examine them." The downside is that a busy schedule leaves little time to do everything she would like to do. As she says, "There's a lot of paperwork. It would be nice if there were less paperwork and more time to work on scholarly things. Research is important."

Of course, it's every assistant curator's hope to move up the curatorial ladder, working toward the additional money and prestige that accompany a promotion. In many cases, a curator would have to be willing to change locations in order to move ahead. But opportunities can be limited, and sometimes it's better to stay right where you are.

Erica explains the situation: "We have one of the two best collections of American paintings in the country—the Metropolitan Museum of Art in New York City has the other—so, you balance the strength of being in an institution that values your field against some of the other things that might not be so positive. In other words, moving to a weaker collection to get a better title. It wouldn't be worth it."

In her opinion, moving to a smaller museum with a smaller collection is not advisable unless you are interested in working toward a career as director. A director of a small museum could eventually move to a directorship at a larger museum, but this career track is more administrative and provides little opportunity for scholarly work.

Advice from a Professional. Erica stresses the need for flexibility, since projects often come up that require workers to juggle several things simultaneously. As she says, "You'll have a couple of different exhibitions you're working on at the same time. One might be coming along in two years, one might be in two months. And you go back and forth between them. Or you'll have three different catalog deadlines for three different shows. You have to write your manuscript and turn it in to the editor. You might get to do a book every five years."

Carolyn Travers—Director of Research

Researchers are the backbone behind every living history museum. Without their efforts, the ability to re-create authentic period characters, to accurately restore historic buildings, or to reproduce a facsimile of daily life would be an impossible task.

Plimoth Plantation consists of four sites: the 1627 Pilgrim Village, the Mayflower II, the Wampanoag Homesite, and the Carriage House Crafts Center. Carolyn Travers is director of research at Plimoth Plantation, and it is her responsibility to ensure that every aspect of each program is thoroughly researched to present as authentic a picture as possible of seventeenth-century life. Her research might include anything, as she says, "from what was the period attitude toward toads, how a character felt about being her husband's third wife, or the correct way to cook a particular dish to some obscure point of Calvinist theology."

Research generally includes the life and genealogical background of a character. According to Carolyn, it is more difficult to research the female characters because there is less documented information available about them than about the males. The researchers use several sources, including court records and genealogical research done by professionals from such organizations as the General Society of Mayflower Descendants or writers for genealogy periodicals.

Other types of research are handled by different departments. For example, re-creating authentic buildings and structures is the responsibility of the curatorial department.

Getting Started. Carolyn attended Earlham College, a small Quaker school in Richmond, Indiana, where she earned a bachelor's degree in fine arts with a concentration in history. She went on to Simmons Graduate School of Library and Information Science in Boston and graduated with a master's degree in library and information science with a concentration in research methods.

She grew up in Plymouth and started work at the age of fourteen as a part-time Pilgrim. After she finished her master's degree, she returned to Plimoth Plantation as a researcher.

Advice from a Professional. Carolyn warns that researching is a competitive field and that an advanced degree is needed, specifically in history or library science with a concentration in research methods. A candidate is not expected to have a general body of knowledge about the specific time period, but he or she must have strong research skills, talent, and experience.

Earnings in Living History Museums. New graduates might begin with a salary in the low twenties. As Carolyn stresses, "You don't do it for the money. There are a lot of psychological payments. One of the satisfactions for me is to be able to change someone's mind about the stereotypes surrounding early colonists."

For Further Reading

The American Association of Museums (AAM) assembles the *Official Museum Directory*, published by National Register Publishing, and it is a valuable resource found in the reference section of most libraries. In addition to its pages and pages of history museums, historic houses, buildings, and sites, it lists scores of historical and preservation societies, boards, agencies, councils, commissions, foundations, and research organizations. You could decide on a region where you'd like to work and then approach your choices with a phone call, resume and cover letter, or personal visit.

The AAM also publishes *Museum News*, a bimonthly magazine written by and for museum professionals. It contains information on such issues as leadership, curatorship, marketing and funding, security, ethics, and politics. *Aviso* is the association's monthly e-newsletter. It covers museums in the news, federal legislation affecting museums, upcoming seminars and workshops, federal grant deadlines, and AAM activities and services. You can find information about these resources by contacting the association at the address listed in the Appendix.

To learn more about working in museums in Canada, contact the Canadian Museums Association, listed in the Appendix.

A Final Thought

There are far too many museums to include in this single chapter. They comprise an entire culture of learning and scholarly endeavors and provide countless career opportunities. You might use your own research skills to find more information about this interesting field.

CHAPTER EIGHT

Botanical Specialists

otanical gardens and arboretums are parks open to the general public, students, and research scientists. Plants, flowers, trees, and shrubs are collected from all over the world and exhibited in arrangements by family, country of origin, or aesthetics.

Typical visitors to botanical gardens and arboretums fall into six categories: dedicated professional scientists and horticulturists who utilize the gardens' collections for research purposes or to identify specific plants; professional and amateur gardeners who participate in adult education classes and training programs; horticultural students enrolled in internship programs through their universities; local residents who come to enjoy a peaceful sanctuary; schoolchildren and their teachers; and international travelers and scientists interested in the collections and histories of the gardens.

Botanical gardens and arboretums generally offer public programs such as classes in gardening, question-and-answer hotlines to help with gardening problems, tours of the grounds, and lectures on the various collections.

Although not all, most botanical gardens and arboretums are involved with ongoing research issues. Curators and other horticulturists go on collection trips to add to the types of plants in their gardens and to study the plant life in other geographic regions.

Living plants are added to the grounds, and pressed and dried plants are stored in herbaria and are shared with researchers all over the world.

Employment Options

There are many positions in botanical gardens and arboretums that would be of interest to scholars. Although job titles can vary from institution to institution, some of the common designations follow.

ADMINISTRATION AND FACILITIES

- **Director.** Provides leadership and is responsible for policy making, funding, planning, organizing, staffing, and directing activities throughout the institution.
- **Assistant Director.** Responsible for operations, which may include finance, personnel, security, safety, and maintenance of facilities.
- **Business Manager.** Responsible for accounting, payroll, purchasing, personnel, and financial record keeping.

HORTICULTURE, CURATION OF COLLECTIONS

- **Head of Horticulture.** Directs the horticultural function of the institution, including the management of staff, programs, activities, and plant collections.
- **Curator of Horticulture.** Advises on care of plant collections and acquisitions.
- **Plant Records Keeper.** Maintains inventory of plants. Processes acquisitions, accession and deaccession, mapping, relocating, and labeling.
- **Production Supervisor.** Supervises the growing of plants in the nursery.
- **Propagator.** Propagates plant materials for collections.

GROUNDS MANAGEMENT

- **Horticulture Supervisor.** Supervises garden workers, plans and schedules work assignments, and is responsible for equipment.

- **Foreman.** Directs labor crews in general groundskeeping tasks.
- **Gardener.** Responsible for the maintenance of a specialized plant area or collection.
- **Arborist.** Responsible for the care of trees, including trimming, transplanting, and removal.

EDUCATION, VISITOR SERVICES

- **Head of Education.** Responsible for several departments or programs. Supervises several education professionals and/or volunteers.
- **Education Specialist.** Responsible for a specific program. Supervises staff related to that program.
- **Visitor Services Manager.** Coordinates informational programs and services.

Training

If you ask botanical garden or arboretum professionals what kind of training they think you'll need, most are likely to recommend a college internship as the way to get started. Not only will an internship provide you with contacts for future employment, it will expose you to the different career options available within these settings and help you to define the path you'll need to follow.

Horticulture is a profession that requires work experience and on-the-job training in addition to education. Most employers say they would not hire anyone without work experience, whether it involves summer jobs or an internship program.

Most public gardens offer one or more student internship programs, though they might differ in the degree of responsibility and the departments in which the intern could work. Depending on the garden, internships are available in the following areas:

- arboriculture
- continuing education
- curating
- display design
- greenhouse production
- horticulture indoor display
- horticulture research
- integrated pest management
- library science
- marketing
- nursery
- outdoor display
- performing arts
- planning and design
- student programs
- visitor education

Internships can run from three months to a year and may include a stipend. Aside from the actual work, the internship may also include learning activities, such as lectures and field trips. Occasional weekend, evening, and holiday work may be required. Student housing may be available.

Professional Gardener Training Program

Longwood Garden's tuition-free two-year internship program is offered every other year and is open to those with a high school diploma and at least one year of experience in garden work. Students work three days a week in all horticultural areas of the garden and receive classroom instruction from Longwood staff and outside instructors two days per week. They also rotate as the supervisor of a student work crew, which helps develop management skills. As in the college internship program, students receive a taxable stipend of $8.50 per hour, and housing is available.

Students work at one-month rotations in each of eight major indoor and outdoor areas: arboriculture, indoor display, production, groundskeeping, outdoor display, research, integrated pest management, and curatorial.

Graduates of the Professional Gardener Training Program are sought after by employers such as public gardens, commercial horticulture companies, and estate gardens.

Salaries

Salaries in the botanical specialties vary depending on your level of education and amount of experience, as well as on the area of the country in which you work.

In general, entry-level workers in groundskeeping positions receive hourly wages, usually beginning at around $10 per hour. Salaries are higher for employees trained in applying pesticides and pruning trees.

According to the American Institute for Biological Science, the 2003 median salary for plant biologists with less than one year of experience was $33,000. For all positions without supervisory responsibilities, the median was $48,000. Workers who supervise other employees and those with more extensive experience earned more than $100,000.

Profiles

Some botanical scholars have shared their stories with us. Read the following accounts to see whether their experiences match your interests. You'll also learn about two interesting settings where these professionals work.

Longwood Gardens

Longwood Gardens is located in Kennett Square, Pennsylvania, a suburb of Philadelphia. It is really more of a display garden than a botanic garden. Although there are many plants that could be called collections, they exist for the sake of the landscape, which is how it differs from a traditional botanic garden. There is much more emphasis on the art of the landscape than on the actual study of the plants themselves. In a botanical garden, on the other hand, the emphasis is usually on collecting plants and keeping data on them for the purpose of display and study.

Pierre Dupont, the founder of Longwood Gardens, was interested in creating a mood and a sense of place that would allow people to interact within a garden setting. Even though he had many unusual and beautiful specimens, his main emphasis was on the art of horticulture and the setting he was creating.

The horticultural division at Longwood Gardens contains a research component. Here scholars try to bring science to bear on display horticulture. The scientists use their knowledge to help the staff be efficient, imaginative, and responsible to the environment in fabricating the plant displays.

Longwood Gardens is also a historic garden. It includes an arboretum started by a Quaker family who received a land grant from William Penn, whom Pennsylvania is named for. They planted trees in the 1780s that still exist, and it was that core arboretum that was the compelling factor in Pierre Dupont's decision to buy the property. The trees were due to be logged, and Dupont bought the land to save them, ultimately developing Longwood Gardens around it.

Dupont was an engineer who had a love of water in the garden, so he built fountain gardens that were inspired by his visits to Europe. There is a theater garden where live performances are held, and the curtain is a curtain of water jets.

There is also a topiary garden of abstract shapes, and many old trees, grand vistas, and monumental architecture at the conservatories, with bronze windows and mica-shaded lamps inside.

Rick Darke—Curator of Plants

Rick Darke served on the staff of Longwood Gardens for twenty years—eleven as curator of plants. He has a bachelor's degree in plant sciences from the University of Delaware, and he also studied art and anthropology before deciding on his major.

Getting Started. Rick's first job was as an intern at Longwood, and he later moved up to assistant taxonomist (taxonomy is the science of classifying organisms). He took graduate courses but ended up having the opportunity to take over a doctoral position in taxonomy that was rewritten as curator of plants. When the man Rick worked for announced that he would retire in two years, Rick had to choose between continuing in a graduate program or staying on the job and developing the skills he'd need to take over the position. He chose to stay, and it was a good decision.

The Work. One of Rick's main responsibilities as curator of plants was to oversee the identification, mapping, and labeling of plants done by the curatorial assistants working under his supervision. Identifying and labeling every item grown is one of the most important tasks at Longwood Gardens.

Rick participated regularly on landscape and advisory committees, making recommendations and working with teams of colleagues to create and restore the gardens. His role was to suggest plants that could be used in place of existing plantings or to comment on architectural details or other design elements.

As a curator, he traveled extensively while working at Longwood. He visited Australia, New Zealand, Japan, South Africa, Brazil, England, and Germany, bringing plants from different climates back from each trip. Longwood Gardens includes a four-acre area under glass where the staff can create specialized environments for plants from other climates.

Rick's duties included a considerable amount of teaching. Longwood offers several programs for students, and he regularly taught a botany course in the Professional Gardener Training Program, as well as other classes for graduate students. He also taught courses for the continuing education program, including evening lectures and field trips, and led tours to native areas and other gardens.

Rick is also a writer. He contributed to the Longwood Garden's in-house publication and wrote magazine articles about the happenings at Longwood. For example, he traveled to Brazil and worked with a landscape architect there whom he brought back to Pennsylvania. The architect created a garden at Longwood, and Rick wrote an article about it, collaborating with a photographer to publicize a celebration of the gardens at Longwood.

What Rick enjoyed most was the eclectic mix of his job and his interaction with students. There was usually an intern working in his office, and he was also regularly teaching people as they moved through the organization. Over the years, he made a strong network of friends and professional colleagues across the country and throughout the world.

Since leaving Longwood Gardens, Rick has served as a horticultural consultant for public gardens and landscapes. His clients include the Chicago Botanic Garden, the Rio Grande Botanic Garden, and Baltimore's Druid Hill Conservatory. He lectures nationally on topics related to horticulture and landscape architecture and is an active freelance writer and photographer. His books include *The American Woodland Garden: Capturing the Spirit of the Deciduous Forest* (Timber Press, 2002), *In Harmony with Nature: Lessons from the Arts and Crafts Garden* (Jason Denmark, 2000), and *The Encyclopedia of Grasses for Livable Landscapes* (Timber Press, 2007).

Advice from a Professional. Rick says that to succeed as a curator of plants, you need skills in addition to your love of plants. Strong writing and verbal skills are very important because you interact with many different people. He stresses that he would not have been able to do his job well without the ability to communicate clearly and to teach others.

The Arnold Arboretum

The Arnold Arboretum is located in Jamaica Plain, Massachusetts, a section of Boston, and is affiliated with Harvard University. Its mission is the biology, cultivation, and conservation of temperate woody plants and includes continuing research, education, and community outreach work. The Arnold Arboretum was established in 1874 by Harvard botanist Asa Gray. It began with 123 species of neglected woody plants and has grown to include 265 beautifully maintained acres, with approximately fifteen thousand plants in its living collection.

Chris Strand—Outreach Horticulturist

Chris Strand is an outreach horticulturist at the Arnold Arboretum. He earned his bachelor's degree in biology from the University of Colorado, Boulder, concentrating on taxonomy, the study of the different species and how they are classified.

After graduation, he won a fellowship sponsored by Longwood Gardens and earned his master's degree in public horticulture at the University of Delaware in Newark. He worked for one year at Callaway Gardens near Atlanta, Georgia, before coming to the Arnold Arboretum.

The Work. Chris is in charge of visitor services, a position with a wide range of duties. He develops and manages the exhibits that are shown in the exhibit hall, where information is passed on to visitors through an information desk, a photographic display, and a bookstore. He trains the volunteers who are stationed in the hall to answer visitors' questions, ensures that the bookstore buyer has everything needed for the exhibit, and sees that maps of the grounds are available so visitors can find their way around the arboretum.

Chris also teaches in the adult education program. He covers woody plant identification and teaches a six-week course on the highlights of the arboretum. He describes his students as people with varied interests in continuing education; they include retired people, volunteers wanting to learn more about the plants, and rangers from the National Park Service. (The Arnold Arboretum maintains a cooperative arrangement with the National Park

Service through which interpretive rangers are taught to conduct historical landscape restoration and maintenance.)

Chris also works with a consultant on an ongoing project to improve signage on the grounds. In addition, he answers requests for information about the arboretum and requests for publications. He supervises volunteers who run a plant answer line once a week and supplies them with the materials they need for the job.

The part of his job that Chris most enjoys is spending time among the collections. "My boss has made it clear that I'm supposed to be very familiar with everything," he says, "so I spend a lot of time going outside, looking at plants, photographing them, learning about them. We have well over eleven thousand different specimens on the grounds, and the best part is that I always have the opportunity to learn more about them."

What he likes least is dealing with difficult people. Chris observes that since the Arnold Arboretum is a public park and does not charge admission, people occasionally disregard the rules. Some bring unleashed dogs or take cuttings from the plants.

Climbing the Career Ladder in Public Horticulture. Graduate programs in public horticulture are directed toward people who are interested in working in education or administration. Chris plans to continue working in public horticulture, hoping to eventually be in charge of a public program at an arboretum or botanical garden. Wherever his career takes him, though, he hopes to always have direct contact with the plants because they are what he loves most about his work.

Susan Kelley—Curatorial Associate

Susan Kelley is a curatorial associate for the living collections at Arnold Arboretum. Her job involves mapping the living specimens on the grounds and labeling each plant. She earned bachelor's and master's degrees in music before deciding to change careers. She then earned a master's in plant population from City

University of New York and worked at the Harvard University Herbaria until she applied for her position at Arnold Arboretum.

The Work. Mapping and labeling are an important part of the work done at Arnold. Along with being a horticultural garden, the arboretum is also a research facility. Visitors from many countries use the collections for study purposes, so maps showing where each individual specimen is located have been kept for more than seventy years.

Susan was heavily involved in the arboretum's switch from hand-drawn maps to a computerized mapping system. Her role in this huge project was to transcribe the hand-drawn maps to the computerized versions and also to maintain current hand-drawn maps until the new system was completed.

There are two major plantings each year, in the spring and fall, when about a thousand new plants are added to the grounds. It is Susan's responsibility to put all of these new plantings on the maps. She makes sure that every plant is labeled, a procedure that involves hanging two labels directly on the plant to provide an accession number, the name of the plant, the family, where it came from, and its map location.

Susan's work with a plant begins when it goes from the nursery to the grounds. She prepares the labels, which are the size of credit cards and made of aluminum, by embossing the required information from the arboretum's database onto them and then attaching them to the plants.

She also performs field checks of each individual specimen to determine its condition. She recommends replacement of damaged or unhealthy plants to the horticultural taxonomist and informs the propagator if a specimen needs to be repropagated.

Working outside is one of Susan's favorite things about her job. "What I love most is being outdoors in this great collection of plants," she says. "It's one of the best collections in the world. There are very old specimens, and then we have all these new plants coming in. I also like that I have some indoor work. The computer work I do is challenging mentally. The mix is ideal."

The only stress that Susan experiences comes from the fact that her department is understaffed. She says, "My job is extensive enough that three people should really be doing it." She does have volunteers and two summer interns to help, but training them is time-consuming and adds to her workload.

Susan has a good way to handle occasional stress, however. "Whenever I need to regroup, I can just go outside," she says. "I have a beautiful place in which to do it."

Anne Brennan—Student Intern

Anne Brennan graduated from Penn State with a B.S. in horticulture and worked at Longwood Gardens as a postgraduate intern in the education division. It was a ten-month paid internship that provided a monthly stipend and free housing and gave Anne a chance to experience different career options to help her decide which path to pursue. Here are her recollections of her time at Longwood.

Anne initially considered horticultural production in a greenhouse or nursery as a possible career. However, she realized that there are so many other options than just growing plants, an observation that was reinforced during her internship, when she saw new opportunities every day.

Since botanical gardens weren't emphasized in her college studies, Anne was unaware of the career possibilities that exist for horticulturists, educators, publicists, groundskeepers, and many other professionals. She observes that this gap in her undergraduate education might be the result of her school's curriculum and teachers who focus on research and academics rather than practical experience and production. Although her advisor frequently suggested graduate school, she wasn't very excited by the idea.

Once she graduated and began her internship at Longwood, Anne saw many other options that better suited her. She worked in the student programs office at Longwood, which coordinates the internship programs, including the Professional Gardener Training Program and an international student internship program. In effect, she worked as an intern coordinating other interns.

Anne's internship included working on various projects that she found interesting. She responded to questions from students interested in the programs. She also helped with rewriting the promotional materials on the programs and organized the orientation program for new interns. In this capacity, she arranged for speakers to address the students, led tours of the grounds, and organized field trips to other botanical gardens.

Good communication skills were an important part of Anne's job because she interacted regularly with forty students in the different areas of the gardens. She attended meetings twice a month and wrote a long weekly memo that served as a newsletter to keep students informed about upcoming activities. Anne was the first person visitors met when they came to the student programs office, and she enjoyed greeting them. She also learned some management skills by running meetings.

Although uncertain about her future plans, Anne expressed interest in garden writing and education. She has some experience working for a horticultural trade magazine and is eager to learn publishing and layout. She is also considering pursuing a full-time career in the education program of a public garden.

For Further Reading

The following resources are publications of the American Public Gardens Association (APGA) and can be ordered directly from the association at the address listed in the Appendix.

- *The Public Garden.* A quarterly journal with themed issues focusing on topics of interest to public horticulture professionals.
- *APGA Salary Survey.* Contains the latest salary and benefit information for twenty-two positions in administration, horticulture, and education at U.S. and Canadian botanical gardens.

A Final Thought

A green thumb can be an excellent starting point for a scholarly career. If you love plants and are interested in pursuing one of the many fields involved in their growth, care, and display, you can find an exciting career as a professional in a botanical garden or arboretums.

CHAPTER NINE

Animal Behaviorists

In addition to the scholarly careers that involve studying humans, plants, and information in general, there is a range of professionals who study animals and their behavior. The ideal animal behaviorist is someone who has experience handling animals and who is professionally trained in the areas of the scientific analysis of behavior, as well as being trained to counsel people about animals.

Employment Options

Many career options exist for an animal behaviorist. Let's look a bit more closely at some of them.

Independent Trainers

Many animal behaviorists work independently and offer training programs to pet owners. If you want to get started on your own, veterinarians are the best referral sources.

Teachers

Some animal behaviorists stay in the academic world, where they conduct research and pass on their knowledge and experience to university-level students. Just as with any professorial post, you need a doctorate and must meet the specific requirements of the hiring department.

Animal-Assisted Therapists

Another career option is animal-assisted therapy, in which animals become part of the therapeutic process. They can be used to help people with a wide range of needs, such as a social dog for a child with emotional or social problems, or a dog that acts as a prosthesis, such as Seeing Eye, hearing ear, or seizure-alert dogs, for example. Animal behaviorists train animals for these roles.

For example, Dr. Mary Lee Nitschke (see her profile later in this chapter) teaches others about hippotherapy, which involves working with horses to help humans with neuromuscular difficulties. Hippotherapy is horseback riding directed by a physical therapist or kinesiologist, where the movement of the horse is used as a way of stimulating neuromuscular interaction patterns in the rider. Dr. Nitschke's goal is to teach people in the medical field about the many possibilities that are available therapeutically with animals. "I hope I'm carving out a path that will become more common as the years go by—teaching people to use animals therapeutically," she says.

Another application of animal-assisted therapy is showcased by the work of Dr. Mary Birch, who works with babies who were born addicted to crack cocaine. These infants have no inhibitory control and scream most of the time, making it very hard for the nurses to care for them. It is also very difficult to have an impact on them in any way.

Dr. Birch uses a concept called entrainment, in which the rhythm that occurs in the patient is matched to a corresponding rhythm, with the goal of bringing down the higher rhythm of the patient. She started with little, active finches in a cage right next to the baby, who is eventually entrained on the birds. Then she substituted the finches with birds that moved more slowly, to the point where she could finally use a chinchilla to soothe the baby. The concept combines biofeedback, animal behavior, and circadian rhythm. These are just some examples of the many ways that animal behavior can be used therapeutically.

Medical Researchers

As any animal lover knows, research using animals is a controversial subject, to say the least. An animal behaviorist working with scientists for the betterment of animals can ensure that humane practices are followed.

Animal Training Instructors

Teaching other people how to train animals is a viable career path for animal behaviorists. Although the notion of training animals for circuses or television or film work might be abhorrent to some (there are many who believe that animals should be left in the wild and not used for any purposes related to people's needs), animals can humanely be trained to interact with humans in a therapeutic setting.

Zoo Specialists

Many zoos hire animal behaviorists or work with consultants to train zookeepers how to handle and interact well with the animals. More and more zoos operate open park facilities as opposed to keeping animals in cement-floored cages. Animal behaviorists teach zoo owners about the needs of the different animals—for example, which animals can be kept in the same park spaces together and which must be kept separated.

Training

The ability to think critically is probably one of the most valuable assets an animal behaviorist should have. That also includes the ability to evaluate—to be able to tell what the results you see mean and to evaluate them without reference to your personal prejudices. Some animal behaviorists earn a doctorate degree in animal behavior programs in university psychology or zoology departments. They also must combine hands-on experience with their research interests.

Salaries

Salaries vary widely depending on the specific work you do and the area in which you live. Those working for a university would expect to be on the same pay scale as any other faculty member of the same rank and experience, ranging from about $46,000 for lecturers to more than $90,000 for full professors.

Those who work independently, whether as trainers or teachers, can set their own fees. Most charge an hourly rate for animal training, and a set fee for classes. In general, rates start at about $100 per hour.

Profile

Perhaps the best way to learn about this interesting career is to hear from an experienced professional. Read on to learn more about one scholar's experiences and background.

Mary Lee Nitschke—Animal Behaviorist

Mary Lee Nitschke has a Ph.D. in comparative developmental psychobiology from Michigan State University and more than thirty years of experience in this exciting field. She feels that the most important training for an animal behaviorist is hands-on experience, and the more time spent observing animals and learning to interact with them, the better. In addition, she recommends formal education that teaches you to understand, evaluate, and think like a scientist.

In her opinion, the best approach is to take a lot of experimental courses in psychology or in other fields. Some anthropology courses are good preparation for this kind of work, and there are disciplines of animal behavior in both psychology and zoology. A good psychology background is important because it will expose you to experimental psychology and statistics.

Dr. Nitschke uses applied statistics on a daily basis. "I'll give you an example," she says. "Every time a client comes in to me and says 'this is happening,' in my mind I run that through a statistical analysis, and I say, given that situation, what is the probability this is happening for these reasons. That's where my training and my knowledge of animal behavior allows me to put that in a framework instantly."

Getting Started. Dr. Nitschke grew up on the range in Texas, where her primary entertainment and stimulation came from observing animals. She spent a great deal of time with animals, particularly showing and training horses. When she started college, she was attracted to both engineering and psychology because she loved both machines and animal behavior.

She was very interested in the realization that her theoretical learning in psychology seemed to be wasted if it wasn't applied. She found that her professors knew very little about training and were teaching learning theory. On the other hand, trainers knew nothing about learning theory. She believed that both of these areas could be enriched by the other, and she kept bouncing back and forth between the world of training and the world of academics. When she got to graduate school and discovered that she could actually study this as an academic subject, she was fascinated with putting the two together.

Most of her research in graduate school was aimed at the interspecific communication of distress. For her dissertation, she conducted research with bobwhite quail, jackrabbits, coyotes, blue jays, and human babies, looking for whether there was some universality of understanding of the distress call between species.

After graduation, Dr. Nitschke taught at Michigan State University. Her subjects included operant behavior and pet communication patterns in the veterinary school. She also taught developmental psychobiology with a specialization in toxicology, again looking across species at the common elements in how toxins affect behavior in various species.

"Before I even went to college, I trained horses," she says. "What I later realized is that I trained every animal I came into contact with—I just didn't realize that's what it was called.

"While I was an undergraduate, one of the things that fueled my interest in applied psychology was that I started out working in a kennel that bred and trained collies. It was really one of the golden fortunes of my life that the couple I worked for had incredible integrity and ethics about breeding. They bred for the love of the dog and could not be bought by local fashions and current fads. They knew exactly what they were breeding for—solid temperaments. I learned an incredible amount from them. I started there just cleaning dog runs, and by the time I left I was handling the line of collies professionally."

The Work. Dr. Nitschke wears many hats. She is a full-time, tenured professor in the psychology department at Linfield College in Portland, Oregon. Her courses range from Applied Animal Behavior and Human Animal Relationships to People Pet Partnerships in Health Care. She is also owner of Animal School Incorporated (in Beaverton, Oregon) and, through private consultations and classes, provides clients with help in solving pet behavior problems.

Here is an example of the kinds of problems she sees. "Recently, a fellow came in with a six-year-old bulldog mix. It looked an awful lot like a pit bull—big dog, ninety pounds, and he has bitten about seven people. I went through each bite. Some of these bites are almost to be expected because they resulted from inappropriate behavior on the part of the owner. In one instance, the owner sent a plumber carrying a pipe into the dog's territory without announcing him. Well, he already knew the dog was territorial and didn't usually admit strangers. I don't count that bite. That was to be expected. In another instance, a teenage boy had been playing with the dog, then turned very abruptly and jumped on his bike, and the dog went for him. Given this particular dog, the probability of that happening is pretty high, and, when you add all those bites up, the probability that the dog is going to bite again is also very high. Putting the dog to sleep is one of the major options I counseled him about, but you can't make that decision for the client. My job in that situation is to say, here are the likely scenarios—what will happen if you do nothing or if you do this, that, or the other."

What the owner wanted was a training program that would guarantee that the dog wouldn't bite anyone again, but Dr. Nitschke explains that there is no such program. Most of the time you're working with the person, not the animal, and that's why you must have some grounding in counseling to do this work.

Dr. Nitschke is also a consultant to the Oregon Zoo in Portland. She works with the zoo's full-time animal behaviorist, running training seminars for zookeepers on how to interact with and handle animals.

She also gives talks on wolf-dog crosses because the zoo gets many questions about them. Since the zoo has wolves, people bring their concerns about their own pets, and she helps to answer the questions. Many people living in the Northwest own wolves as pets, which can be a dangerous situation. To an animal behaviorist such as Dr. Nitschke, the biggest problem is the quality of life for the animal. If it's high percentage wolf, it's likely to be terrified of people and unpredictable. There is no way of knowing when the wolf part is going to be operative and when the dog part is. These wolf-dog crosses have a reputation very similar to pit bulls and rottweilers. Although it's not the same problem, it looks the same because they maul children frequently.

Dr. Nitschke also does training with the zookeepers, teaching them to manage animals in the zoo environment and to understand and use operant behavior and clicker training, in which the animal is trained to click a bar that delivers food as a reward. One of her colleagues was working with an ape that was diabetic and needed to have a blood sample drawn every day. Through clicker training, she taught the chimp to put its arm in a sleeve outside the cage and grasp a bar so that the blood sample could be taken quickly and efficiently without endangering anyone. The reward was food, and the animal was fine about it.

This colleague also taught an elephant to present its feet for cleaning through a fence. This was an aggressive male elephant that would not allow anyone to enter its territory for cleaning. Through operant conditioning, it was taught to hold its feet up to a little panel where they could be cleaned.

In addition, Dr. Nitschke does a lot of public speaking and is also a consultant for the invisible fencing industry. She also does occasional training for animal-control workers, teaching them how to handle animals and how to approach an animal when they have to go onto a property, which is extremely dangerous.

For Further Reading

There are many books available on different aspects of animal behavior. Here are a few titles to start you on your search for additional information.

Bolhuis, Johan J., and Luc-Alain Giraldeau, Eds. *The Behavior of Animals: Mechanisms, Function and Evolution.* New York: Wiley, 2004.

Gould, James L., and Carol G. Gould. *Animal Architects: Building and the Evolution of Intelligence.* New York: Basic Books, 2004.

Williams, Marta. *Learning Their Language: Intuitive Communication with Animals and Nature.* Novato, CA: New World Library, 2003.

A Final Thought

You can see that animal behavior is a vast field, with many opportunities for challenging and fulfilling careers. If you love animals and are comfortable working with them, you might direct your scholarly endeavors toward the wild kingdom and find the perfect job for your interests.

CHAPTER TEN

Researchers, Writers, and Genealogists

esearch is a major interest of most scholars and a large component of many of the jobs covered in this book. Whether they are involved in their own research or depend on the findings of others for their work, most scholars rely heavily on research in any of a variety of fields. As you have seen throughout this book, university professors, curators, archivists, and anthropologists, to name just a few, involve themselves in some way with research activity.

In this chapter you will learn about scholars whose careers are built on their skills as researchers and writers. You'll also learn about the field of genealogy, which is an interesting example of a career that requires a combination of strong research and writing skills and that also lends itself to freelancing. In addition, you will read the accounts of a professional writer and two freelance researchers.

Researchers and Writers

Writers develop original fiction and nonfiction for a variety of sources, including books, magazines, trade journals, online publications, company newsletters, radio and television broadcasts, motion pictures, and advertisements. Wherever their work appears, the one characteristic that all writers share is the ability to thoroughly conduct research. Whether writing a novel, a newspaper article, or a biography, a writer must be able to locate the information needed by researching every possible resource and then organize and interpret it for the readers. All writers, especially those who write nonfiction, rely on their research skills to establish their credibility with editors and readers.

Some writers specialize in fields that require specific research skills, such as technical writers or science and medical writers. Technical writers put technical information into easily understandable language, working on projects such as operating and maintenance manuals, catalogs, parts lists, assembly instructions, sales promotion materials, and project proposals. Many work with engineers on technical subject matters to prepare written interpretations of engineering and design specifications and other information.

Science and medical writers prepare a range of formal documents presenting detailed information on the physical or medical sciences. They convey research findings for scientific or medical professions and organize information for advertising or public relations needs. Many work with researchers on technical subjects to prepare written interpretations of data and other information for the general public.

Most writers and researchers are familiar with technology, and many couldn't imagine working without laptop computers, desktop or electronic publishing systems, scanners, and software that helps them to organize their material. Some writers prepare material directly for the Internet, which may include writing for electronic newspapers or magazines, creating short fiction or poetry, or producing technical documentation that is available only online. Those who write text for websites are comfortable working with graphic design, page layout, and multimedia software.

Nonfiction writers either propose a topic or are assigned one by an editor or publisher. Combining their research skills with personal observation and interviews, they select and organize the material they want to use to express ideas and convey information in the final piece.

Freelance writers work independently. They write novels, nonfiction books, magazine and newspaper articles, and advertising copy, selling their work to the appropriate clients. Some contract with a publisher to write a book or an article; others are hired to complete specific assignments, such as writing about a new product or technology.

Genealogists

In the last several years, the study of genealogy, tracing family histories, has become one of the most popular hobbies in the United States. More and more people are becoming interested in their family backgrounds. Many genealogy hobbyists take their interest one step further and become self-employed genealogists, helping others to fill out the leaves of their family trees.

Genealogists are also employed in historical societies and libraries with special genealogy rooms. The Church of Jesus Christ of Latter-Day Saints in Salt Lake City, for example, has a huge repository of family information in a subterranean library and maintains an extensive database of genealogical records. The church employs genealogists all over the world, including many who have been accredited through its own program on a list of freelance researchers. You can request information from the Accreditation Program of the Family History Library at the address listed in the Appendix.

Other genealogists find work teaching their skills in adult education classes, editing genealogy magazines, or writing books or newspaper genealogy columns.

How to Get Started

The National Genealogy Society makes the following suggestions for beginners:

1. **Question older family members.** Encourage them to talk about their childhoods and relatives and listen carefully for clues they might inadvertently drop. Learn good interviewing techniques so you ask questions that elicit the most productive answers. Use a tape recorder or video recorder and try to verify each fact through a separate source.

2. **Visit your local library.** Become familiar with historical and genealogical publications and contact local historical societies and the state library and archives in your state capital. Seek out any specialty ethnic or religious libraries and visit cemeteries.

3. **Visit courthouses.** Cultivate friendships with busy court clerks. Ask to see source records such as wills, deeds, marriage books, and birth and death certificates.

4. **Enter into correspondence.** Contact other individuals or societies involved with the same families or regions. Contact foreign embassies in Washington, D.C. Restrict yourself to asking only one question in each letter or e-mail you send. Include the information you have already uncovered. Include a self-addressed, stamped envelope to encourage replies.

5. **Use the Internet.** Members of the National Genealogical Society can participate in a special computer interest section that encourages the use of computers in research, record management, and data sharing.

6. **Keep painstaking records.** Use printed family group sheets or pedigree charts. Develop a well-organized filing system so you'll be able to easily find your information. Keep separate records for each family you research. Special software packages are available to help you keep track of all

of your records, and websites such as Anecestry.com and Genealogy.com offer extensive resources for your search.

7. **Contact the National Genealogical Society.** The organization offers publications such as *Genealogy 101: How to Trace Your Family's History and Heritage* and *Planting Your Family Tree Online: How to Create Your Own Family History Website.* The society also offers a home study course and online courses.

Although most genealogists are not formally trained, specializing in genealogy is possible through some university history and library science programs. Board certification is also an option. For information on certification requirements and procedures, contact the Board for Certification of Genealogists. The address is listed in the Appendix.

Salaries

In 2004, salaried writers had median earnings of $44,350, with most earning between $31,720 and $62,930. Median earnings were $54,410 in advertising and related services and $37,010 in newspaper, periodical, book, and directory publishing.

According to the Society for Technical Communication, the median annual salary for entry-level technical writers was $42,500 in 2004.

Salaries of genealogists vary depending on the institution where they work and on the level of expertise he or she has attained. Most self-employed genealogists earn anywhere from $25 to $50 an hour.

Profiles

Two freelance researchers and a professional novelist have shared their accounts. Read on to learn about their interesting careers.

Valarie Neiman—Academic Researcher

Valarie Neiman formed EVN Flow Services in 1993. Through her home-based business, she does academic, business, and creative writing and provides research and editing services. She earned her bachelor's degree in business administration (transportation) from Arizona State University in Tempe and her master's in human resources development from Ottawa University in Phoenix.

"Research isn't what I do, it's part of who I am," Valarie explains. "As one of the original latchkey kids in the 1950s, I spent a lot of time reading when I got home from school. To avoid being bored in class, I'd always read ahead in the textbooks."

Getting Started. Her first job after high school was typing resumes. Eventually her boss began to let Valarie write them, and soon she was also conducting interviews. After working in a variety of clerical and secretarial jobs, she returned to school in her mid-twenties and earned a bachelor's degree in business. Later, while working for a major defense contractor, she began studying for her master's. When she was let go by the employer who had been paying her tuition, she started to work in temporary positions, from management consultant to typist.

Valarie's final temp assignment was researching and writing warehouse procedures, and she convinced the manager that it would be less expensive to hire her as an independent contractor than to pay the temp agency. At the same time, she put up a notice at her alma mater offering to help students with their research projects.

When she began EVN Flow (Ellwood and Valarie Neiman keep work flowing), she expected to help students format and type papers. But she soon found that many adult learners (twenty-five and older) haven't had training or don't remember how to write research papers, and her work soon evolved into filling in the gaps in their abilities. Valarie says that part of the job is reassuring clients that they aren't stupid and letting them know that she has developed a unique (and marketable) talent for pulling their work together into a package that makes them look good.

She tutors adult learners in planning, researching, and writing academic papers. She also edits master's research and graduation review projects and is under contract with Ottawa University to read and edit first drafts of master's candidates' theses.

In addition, she collaborates on researching and writing a series of booklets on pricing, niche marketing, networking, outsourcing, tax tips, and how to start a home-based business (published by the Home-Based Business Council of Arizona).

Valarie finds her work enjoyable because every day is different and every project leads her in a new direction. She prefers to work alone, without supervision, focusing on the task at hand until its completion, when she can move on to the next project.

"People may think of researchers as scientists or academics," Valarie says. "I believe research is an element in almost every job, whether dealing with things, people, or ideas. Most of the time, though, it isn't thought of as research.

"To me, the distinction of a job as a researcher is that the goal is to present knowledge in a different way, consolidate facts and assemble them to make a point, discover new relationships in existing knowledge, or develop background and authenticity—in creative writing, for example."

One of the things Valarie likes least about her work is that it isn't full-time and can be seasonal—although the part-time nature of the work is also one of the things she likes best. She began writing a novel to fill those unbillable hours and explains that, by her own choice, she earns enough to pay business expenses and to pay herself a small stipend. Fortunately, travel, postage, supplies, and capital equipment associated with writing are all considered tax-deductible expenses.

Valarie shares a large office at home with her husband, who is her financial manager. She can use her time however she wishes.

Since she likes variety and big projects, she often works for an hour or so on one, then shifts to another, and so forth. On some days, she catches up on phone calls or maintenance, but always remains focused on paying clients. She occasionally works up to fourteen hours a day and some days works for only three or four hours.

Advice from a Professional. Valarie offers some very specific advice: "Read, read, read, research, research, research. Go to the library, get online, practice finding things. Interview people, create questionnaires, read magazines.

"The key requirement for a life of research is a desire, not to say compulsion, to know. In addition, a researcher (whether scientific, academic, or journalistic) needs persistence, judgment, empathy, and intuition. A researcher must establish limits and develop shortcuts, or the process goes on forever, each step leading to another source, ad infinitum."

Based on her own experience, Valarie believes that a researcher with broad experience is more likely to be exposed to a variety of information sources. She has worked in government, major corporations, and small businesses, and each job provided a new set of resources that she is now able to draw upon.

She advises that, while there are many possible ways to get a research job, chances are that you won't find one by answering a classified ad. Researcher is more an activity than a job title, so it's important to network, create an excellent resume, and research your prospects. She does recommend a college degree, up to and including a Ph.D. or postdoctoral experience. The academic major doesn't really matter, since a student who thrives in any academic environment will likely have the curiosity and temperament to excel as a researcher.

Strong writing skills are also very important, since research is useless without presenting results. Facts are just data, and a successful researcher must be able to interpret the facts and consolidate or extrapolate them into usable information.

Finally, Valarie says, "And remember, in scientific or social research, especially, the honesty and ethics of a researcher must be unquestioned. A researcher must maintain the confidentiality of people and ideas."

Susan Broadwater-Chen—Information Specialist and Freelance Writer

Susan Broadwater-Chen owns Moonstone Research and Publications, her home-based business in Charlottesville, Virginia. She has a bachelor's degree in humanities from Asbury College in Wilmore, Kentucky, and a master's in theological studies from Emory University in Atlanta, Georgia.

"I have an insatiable curiosity about just about everything, and I love to write," she says. "I especially like the challenge of having to find something and the excitement that comes when I find it. I love libraries, books, and puzzles, and some of the searches that I do are very much like putting puzzles together."

Getting Started. Susan attended Mountain Empire Community College in Southwest Virginia, taking as many computer courses as possible, including programming. After finishing those courses, she took a job at the University of Virginia (UVA) as a program support technician, and part of her job was to do a lot of editing and spend time working with research assistants.

She eventually took courses through UVA on how to navigate the Internet and create Web pages. She worked at UVA for ten years and ran a business out of her home, doing everything from research to editing.

Susan started her business in 1986 on a part-time, moonlighting basis, and she has been working at it full-time since 1995. When she had built up enough contacts and customers to become independent, she quit her job at UVA and started publishing a monthly newsletter and running a Web page. Once she realized that she could support herself by using her skills to expand her client base, she decided to devote herself full-time to the business.

Susan publishes a monthly newsletter that focuses on Internet materials of use to writers. She also accepts individual research projects from authors who are looking for information that they have difficulty finding on their own.

In addition, she works with some online author colonies or work groups in developing content for research libraries. This includes going through antiquarian books, microfilm, and other sources to provide both primary source materials and bibliographic information. Her company has a storefront on the Internet where writers or anyone else can download some materials for free and pay for others. Susan also offers a clipping service for subscribers and holds a weekly online workshop to help people with questions about finding what they are looking for.

She finds the job demanding, since most clients can't wait a week or two for what they are looking for. In addition, putting out a large newsletter each month and submitting articles to at least one online magazine each month is very time-consuming. The day begins at 6 A.M. with checking e-mail and noting requests while her son has breakfast. Next she checks newsgroups and news services for anything that she'll need to come back to later.

After getting her son on the school bus, she prints the articles she wants to read or save and files them in topical folders. Susan says that you must be organized in this type of work in order to keep paper to a minimum and to know where items are when you need them. She keeps a current folder of things she may want to review or talk about in her newsletter, and the rest is filed by topic.

Next Susan works on the products she intends to sell. This involves reading and writing articles or finding out-of-copyright primary source material that can be edited and reprinted for sale. When this is finished, she turns to the content she is developing for the online services and then checks e-mail again and starts working on the requests she received overnight.

After taking a walk to give herself time away from her desk, she writes at least one review or article for the newsletter and then starts exploring potential Internet sources that she may want to review. She takes notes and makes printouts and puts this information aside to be written up the next day. Then she searches library card catalogs looking for materials to request on interlibrary loan and makes notes on information in those books.

Although working at home means the atmosphere is relaxed, Susan sometimes feels pressured because there seems to be so much to do in a limited amount of time. She usually works about eighty hours a week, which is twice what she did working for someone else. The job is not boring, but it's also hard work.

Susan likes being able to help clients, and she is very pleased when they are happy with what she's found for them. She says, "When I've helped a person who is publishing books and he or she sends me a copy of the book, I get personal satisfaction knowing that I've helped them with the research that the book required. I also like the feeling I get when I find some really obscure fact and pull the needle out of the haystack. The downside is that sometimes I can't help someone because the facts won't bear out what they want to write about."

Advice from a Professional. Based on her experience as a researcher, Susan advises that it's not an easy job. You need to learn all you can about electronic databases and the Internet without forgetting the basic skills of library research and interviewing.

Although the options for Internet research seem infinite, she recommends that you can't have a successful research business if you rely solely on the Internet. "You have to cultivate as many skills as possible and know where to look for specific material," she says. "It's also important to build up a client base and connections before you take this on full-time. Volunteer to do things for groups who might need your services on the Internet and online services. Submit articles to online publications and start networking with people in professions or with interests who might need your services."

Clay Reynolds—Novelist

Clay Reynolds is the author of half a dozen novels in genres such as psychological suspense, crime, and historical. He has been writing fiction professionally since 1984.

Getting Started. Clay's writing career began for an interesting reason. He had worked in scholarship, research, and literary criticism for several years, but he found himself the sole caregiver of his two young children when his wife worked at night outside the home. Since he couldn't get out to the library for research and needed to be alert for most of the evening, he began writing fiction as a way of occupying the hours after his children were asleep.

He completed two novels, *The Vigil* and *Agatite*, which were published by St. Martin's Press. Clay spent three years researching and writing his third novel, *Franklin's Crossing*, which was published by Dutton in 1992. The publisher entered it in the Pulitzer Prize competition, and *Franklin's Crossing* won the Violet Crown Award and was runner-up for the Spur Award for Best Western Novel. The novel was reissued by Signet in 1993.

He next wrote *Players*, a high-tech psychological thriller with strong crime novel elements, which was first published by Carroll and Graf in 1997 then reissued by Pinnacle in 1998. The novel *Monuments* was published by Texas Tech University Press in 2000.

Between writing novels, Clay has also written and edited several nonfiction books and has published short fiction, poetry, original essays, and scholarly material. One nonfiction book is *20 Questions: Answers for Aspiring Writers*, published by Browden Springs Press in 1998.

For most of his writing career, Clay divided his time between writing and teaching at the University of Texas at Dallas, where the administration was accommodating in allowing him to arrange his schedule so that he would have blocks of time for writing.

Although he's never bored, Clay finds that the work does become tedious at times, especially when he's facing deadlines and feeling the general insecurities that can result from balancing inspiration and talent against craft and ability. He recognizes that writing is a solo occupation and that it is hard work that doesn't respond well to interruptions, distractions, or limitations. He says, "There is no worse enemy of mine than telephone solicitors and telemarketers."

Clay works in a home office, away from television and other distractions. He works exclusively with a computer, which helps to facilitate his other writing and editing work. He generally works eight to twelve hours a day, taking occasional breaks for walks, and he may nap if he can't come up with an idea. He also reads a great deal. If he feels that he's on a roll with something, he might work eighteen to twenty-four hours straight.

"Writer's block is a constant and real companion," Clay says. "It can strike at any time, even in the middle of a sentence. Emotions in writing are very close to the surface and are often very real. They have to be generated and nurtured, but they can never override the intellect. This is hard work, and it requires a daily commitment. Writing is not a hobby. It can be fun—it can be marvelous fun—but it's always work, even when it's the most fun."

Advice from a Professional. Clay recommends a strong command of the language and a solid foundation in the rules of grammar. And he suggests that you read as a vital part of your research "You cannot read enough, even if you do nothing else for every waking minute of the rest of your life," he says. "Read, read, read. Read history, sociology, chemistry, poetry, plays, novels, short stories, quantum physics, geography, psychology, sports accounts, daily newspapers, weekly magazines, monthly journals, and high school yearbooks. Read. Especially read literature. Bestsellers only teach you what's hot, not what's good. You cannot write originally if you don't know what's been written. Then sit down and tell a story. Fiction is a lie with which we tell the truth. Tell your lie. Tell it well. But tell it as a story."

For Further Reading

The areas of freelance researching and writing offer many possibilities, and there are countless resources you can refer to for more information. Here are a few examples of books you might consult.

Bates, Mary Ellen. *Building & Running a Successful Research Business: A Guide for the Independent Information Professional.* Medford, NJ: Information Today, 2003.

Bly, Robert. *Getting Started as a Freelance Writer.* Boulder, CO: Sentient Publications, 2006.

Brewer, Robert. *2008 Writer's Market.* Cincinnati: F&W Publications, 2008.

Mills, Elizabeth S., Ed. *Professional Genealogy: A Manual for Researchers, Writers, Editors, Lecturers, and Librarians.* Baltimore: Genealogical Publishing Company, 2001.

A Final Thought

Working as a writer or researcher can present you with countless career opportunities, particularly if you choose to freelance. Genealogy is only one possibility. You've read about two professionals who turned their love of research and writing into profitable businesses. If you know that your interests lie within the realm of scholarly endeavors but aren't quite sure of the subject area you'd like to pursue, think carefully about your interests and skills. You might be able to turn your interests and talents into a viable business opportunity.

Professional Associations

For more information on the career options covered in this book, contact the appropriate professional associations listed below.

College and University Professors

Professional societies generally provide information on academic and nonacademic employment opportunities in their fields. You can find addresses for professional associations for many academic disciplines in the *Occupational Outlook Handbook*. Another resource is the *Encyclopedia of Associations*, available at your library.

For information about faculty union activities on two- and four-year college campuses, contact:

American Federation of Teachers
555 New Jersey Avenue NW
Washington, DC 20001
www.aft.org

Canadian Teachers' Federation
2490 Don Reid Drive
Ottawa, ON K1H 1E1
Canada
www.ctf-fce.ca

For information on college teaching careers, contact:

American Association of University Professors
1012 Fourteenth Street NW, Suite 500
Washington, DC 20005
www.aaup.org

Canadian Association of University Teachers
2705 Queensview Drive
Ottawa, ON K2B 8K2
Canada
www.caut.ca

Special publications on higher education, available in libraries, list specific employment opportunities for faculty. The major periodical is the *Chronicle of Higher Education.*

Librarians and Archivists

Librarians

For information on librarianship, including a listing of accredited education programs and scholarships or loans, contact:

American Library Association (ALA)
50 East Huron Street
Chicago, IL 60611
www.ala.org

Canadian Library Association
328 Frank Street
Ottawa, ON K2P 0X8
Canada
www.cla.ca

For additional information on a career as a special librarian, write to:

Special Libraries Association
331 South Patrick Street
Alexandria, VA 22314
www.sla.org

Material on careers in information science is available from:

American Society for Information Science and Technology
1320 Fenwick Lane, Suite 510
Silver Spring, MD 20910
www.asis.org

Information on graduate schools of library and information science can be obtained from:

Association for Library and Information Science Education
65 East Wacker Place, Suite 1900
Chicago, IL 60601
www.alise.org

Those interested in a position as a librarian in the federal service should visit the following sites:

Public Service Commission of Canada
www.jobs-emplois.gc.ca

United States Office of Personnel Management
www.usajobs.com

For information on a career as a law librarian, as well as a list of ALA accredited library schools offering programs in law librarianship and scholarship information, contact:

American Association of Law Libraries
53 West Jackson, Suite 940
Chicago, IL 60604
www.aallnet.org

Canadian Association of Law Libraries
PO Box 1570
4 Cataraqui Street, Suite 310
Kingston, ON K7L 5C8
Canada
www.callacbd.ca

For information on employment opportunities as a health science librarian, contact:

Medical Library Association
64 East Wacker Place, Suite 1900
Chicago, IL 60601
www.mlanet.org

Information on requirements and application procedures for jobs in the Library of Congress may be obtained directly from:

Personnel Office
Library of Congress
101 Independence Avenue SE
Washington, DC 20540
www.loc.gov

State library agencies can furnish information on scholarships available through their offices, requirements for certification, and general information about career prospects in the state. Several of these agencies maintain job hot lines that report openings for librarians. State departments of education can furnish information on certification requirements and job opportunities for school librarians.

Archivists

For information on archivists and schools offering courses in archival science, contact:

Association of Canadian Archivists
PO Box 2596, Station D
Ottawa, ON K1P 5W6
Canada
www.archivists.ca

Society of American Archivists
527 South Wells Street, Fifth Floor
Chicago, IL 60607
www.archivists.org

For information about certification for archivists, contact:

Academy of Certified Archivists
90 State Street, Suite 1009
Albany, NY 12207
www.certifiedarchivists.org

Social Scientists

Anthropologists

For information about careers, job openings, grants and fellowships, and schools that offer training in anthropology, contact:

The American Anthropological Association
2200 Wilson Boulevard, Suite 600
Arlington, VA 22201
www.aaanet.org

Canadian Anthropological Society
www.casca.anthropologica.ca

Geographers

Information on preparing for a wide range of careers in geography can be obtained from:

Association of American Geographers
1710 Sixteenth Street NW
Washington, DC 20009
www.aag.org

Historians

Information on careers for students of history is available from:

American Historical Association
400 A Street SE
Washington, DC 20003
www.historians.org

Canadian Historical Association
395 Wellington
Ottawa, ON K1A 0N4
Canada
www.cha-shc.ca

General information on careers for historians is available from:

Organization of American Historians
112 North Bryan Avenue
PO Box 5457
Bloomington, IN 47407
www.oah.org

For additional information on careers for historians, contact:

American Association for State and Local History
1717 Church Street
Nashville, TN 37203
www.aaslh.org

Political Scientists

Information on careers and job openings, including *Careers and the Study of Political Science: A Guide for Undergraduates* (which may be purchased for a small fee, with bulk rates for multiple copies), is available from:

American Political Science Association
1527 New Hampshire Avenue NW
Washington, DC 20036
www.apsanet.org

Canadian Political Science Association
260 Rue Dalhousie, #204
Ottawa, ON K1N 7E4
Canada
www.cpsa-acsp.ca

For information on programs in public affairs and administration, contact:

National Association of Schools of Public Affairs and
  Administration
1029 Vermont Avenue NW, Suite 1100
Washington, DC 20005
www.naspaa.org

. . . .

Archaeologists

For information on careers and educational requirements in archaeology, contact:

Archaeological Conservancy
5301 Central Avenue NE, Suite 902
Albuquerque, NM 87108
www.americanarchaeology.com

Archaeological Institute of America
656 Beacon Street, Sixth Floor
Boston, MA 02215
www.archaeological.org

Canadian Archaeological Association
www.canadianarchaeology.com

Center for American Archeology
Kampsville Archeological Center
PO Box 366
Kampsville, IL 62053
www.caa-archeology.org

Crow Canyon Archaeological Center
23390 Road K
Cortez, CO 81321
www.crowcanyon.org

Earthwatch
3 Clock Tower Place, Suite 100
Box 75
Maynard, MA 01754
www.earthwatch.org

The Smithsonian Institution
Anthropology Outreach Office
National Museum of Natural History
PO Box 37012
Washington, DC 20013
www.anthropology.si.edu

Society for American Archaeology
900 Second Street NE, Suite 12
Washington, DC 20002
www.saa.org

Society for Historic Archaeology
15245 Shady Grove Road, Suite 130
Rockville, MD 20850
www.sha.org

....

Psychologists

For information on careers, educational requirements, financial
assistance, and licensing in all fields of psychology, contact:

American Psychological Association
750 First Street NE
Washington, DC 20002
www.apa.org

Canadian Psychological Association
Canadian Association of School Psychologists
141 Laurier Avenue West, Suite 702
Ottawa, ON K1P 5J3
Canada
www.cpa.ca

For information on careers, educational requirements, and
licensing of school psychologists, contact:

National Association of School Psychologists
4340 East West Highway, Suite 402
Bethesda, MD 20814
www.nasponline.org

Canadian Association of School Psychologists
www.cpa.ca

Information about state licensing requirements is available
from:

Association of State and Provincial Psychology Boards
PO Box 241245
Montgomery, AL 36124
www.asppb.org

Information on traineeships and fellowships also is available from colleges and universities that have graduate departments of psychology.

Museum Curators

The following list of associations can be used as a valuable resource guide in locating additional information about specific careers. Many of the organizations publish newsletters listing job and internship opportunities, and others offer an employment service to members. A quick look at the organizations' names will give you an idea of how large the scope is that museums cover.

Advisory Council on Historic Preservation
1100 Pennsylvania Avenue NW, Suite 803
Washington, DC 20004
www.achp.gov

American Arts Alliance
1211 Connecticut Avenue NW, Suite200
Washington, DC 20036
www.americanartsalliance.org

American Association for the Advancement of Science
1200 New York Avenue NW
Washington, DC 20005
www.aaas.org

American Association for Museum Volunteers
PO Box 9494
Washington, DC 20016
www.ansp.org/hosted/aamv

American Association of Museums
1575 Eye Street NW, Suite 400
Washington, DC 20005
www.aam-us.org

American Institute for Conservation of Historic and Artistic
    Works
1156 Fifteenth Street NW, Suite 320
Washington, DC 20005
http://aic.stanford.edu

Association of African-American Museum
www.blackmuseums.org

Association of Art Museum Directors
120 East Fifty-Sixth Street, Suite 520
New York, NY 10022
www.aamd.org

Association of College and University Museums and Galleries
www.acumg.org

Association of Railway Museums
1016 Rosser Street
Conyers, GA 30012
www.railwaymuseum.org

Association of Science-Technology Centers
1025 Vermont Avenue NW, Suite 500
Washington, DC 20005
www.astc.org

Association of Children's Museums
1300 L Street NW, Suite 975
Washington, DC 20005
www.childrensmuseums.org

Association for Living Historical Farms and Agricultural
  Museums
8774 Route 45 NW
North Bloomfield, OH 44450
www.alhfam.org

Canada Council for the Arts
350 Albert Street
PO Box 1047
Ottawa, ON K1P 5V8
Canada
www.canadacouncil.ca

Canadian Museums Association
280 Metcalfe Street, Suite 400
Ottawa, ON K2P 1R7
Canada
www.museums.ca

Costume Society of America
203 Towne Center Drive
Hillsborough, NJ 08844
www.costumesocietyamerica.com

International Association of Museum Facility Administrators
PO Box 277
Groton, MA 01450
www.iamfa.org

International Council on Monuments and Sites
US/ICOMOS
401 F Street NW, Suite 331
Washington, DC 20001
www.icomos.org/usicomos

International Council on Monuments and Sites
ICOMOS Canada
PO Box 737, Station B
Ottawa, ON K1P 5P8
Canada
http://canada.icomos.org

International Museum Theatre Alliance
www.imtal.org

International Planetarium Society
www.ips-planetarium.org

Museum Computer Network
232-329 March Road
Box 11
Ottawa, ON K2K 2E1
Canada
www.mcn.edu

Museum Education Roundtable
PO Box 15727
Washington, DC 20003
www.mer-online.org

Museum Store Association
4100 East Mississippi Avenue, Suite 800
Denver, CO 80246
www.museumdistrict.com

Museums USA
9719 Natalies Way
Ellicott City, MD 21042
www.museumsusa.org

Natural Science Collections Alliance
1313 Dolley Madison Boulevard, Suite 402
McLean, VA 22101
www.nscalliance.org

Botanical Specialists

For information about a range of careers in the fields of botany and horticulture, contact:

American Public Gardens Association
100 West Tenth Street, Suite 614
Wilmington, DE 19801
www.publicgardens.org

American Society of Consulting Arborists
15245 Shady Grove Road, Suite 130
Rockville, MD 20850
www.asca-consultants.org

International Society of Arboriculture
PO Box 3129
Champaign, IL 61826
www.isa-arbor.com

Tree Care Industry Association
3 Perimeter Road, Unit 1
Manchester, NH 03103
www.tcia.org

Animal Behaviorists

Association of Zoos and Aquariums
8403 Colesville Road, Suite 710
Silver Spring, MD 20910
www.aza.org

Latham Foundation for the Promotion of Humane Education
Latham Plaza Building
1826 Clement Avenue
Alameda, CA 94501
www.latham.org

Researchers, Writers, and Genealogists

Researchers

Association of Professional Researchers for Advancement
401 North Michigan Avenue, Suite 2200
Chicago, IL 60611
www.apra.org

Association of Professional Researchers for
  Advancement–Canada
www.apracanada.ca

Writers

American Society of Journalists and Authors
1501 Broadway, Suite 302
New York, NY 10036
www.asja.org

Authors Guild
31 East 32nd Street, Seventh Floor
New York, NY 10016
www.authorsguild.org

Black Writers Alliance
PO Box 542711
Grand Prairie, TX 75054
www.blackwriters.org

Mystery Writers of America
17 East Forty-Seventh Street, Sixth Floor
New York, NY 10017
www.mysterywriters.org

Genealogists

Board for Certification of Genealogists
PO Box 14291
Washington, DC 20044
www.bcgcertification.org

Family History Library
Church of Jesus Christ of Latter-Day Saints
35 North West Temple Street, Room 344
Salt Lake City, UT 84150
www.familysearch.org

National Genealogical Society
3108 Columbia Pike, Suite 300
Arlington, VA 22204
www.ngsgenealogy.org

About the Author

A full-time writer of career books, Blythe Camenson works hard to help job seekers make educated choices. She firmly believes that with enough information, readers can find long-term, satisfying careers. To that end, she researches traditional as well as unusual occupations, talking to a variety of professionals about what their jobs are really like. In all of her books she includes first-hand accounts from people who reveal what to expect in each occupation.

Camenson was educated in Boston, earning her B.A. in English and psychology from the University of Massachusetts and her M.Ed. in counseling from Northeastern University.

In addition to *Careers for Scholars & Other Deep Thinkers*, she has written more than two dozen books for McGraw-Hill.